KRISTINA
Rihanoff

KRISTINA
Rihanoff

DANCING OUT OF
DARKNESS: MY STORY

JOHN BLAKE

Published by John Blake Publishing Ltd,
3 Bramber Court, 2 Bramber Road,
London W14 9PB, England

www.johnblakebooks.com

www.facebook.com/johnblakebooks ⓕ
twitter.com/jblakebooks ⓣ

This edition published in 2015

ISBN: 978 1 78418 773 6

British Library Cataloguing-in-Publication Data:

A catalogue record for this book is available from the British Library.

Design by www.envydesign.co.uk

Printed in Great Britain by CPI Group (UK) Ltd

1 3 5 7 9 10 8 6 4 2

Papers used by John Blake Publishing are natural, recyclable products made
from wood grown in sustainable forests. The manufacturing processes conform
to the environmental regulations of the country of origin.

Every attempt has been made to contact the relevant copyright-holders,
but some were unobtainable. We would be grateful if the appropriate people could
contact us.

To my mother, the strongest woman I know.

Thank you for giving me this life. Thank you for giving me everything you could, even when your own life was overshadowed by darkness.

I'm always learning from you and it was you who taught me that anything is possible – as long as you don't give up. Nothing and no one can break our bond, a bond that is known only to mothers and daughters. This book is dedicated to you and to all those single mothers for whom nothing is impossible.

With all my love,
Kristina

Contents

Acknowledgements

I would like to say a big thank you to John Blake Publishing for all their work on this project. And also thanks to Abi Smith and everyone at Kruger Cowne agency.

Foreword

It is my privilege to have come to know Kristina through our love of dance and our passion for helping children to stay safe. Her love of children and her devotion to our charity, the Dot Com Children's Foundation, is perhaps a side of her life that will come as a surprise, as it is far from the glamour of the stage and the glitter ball!

I was introduced to Kristina in 2010 by Len Goodman, who was my dance teacher during my childhood, but is perhaps better known as the head judge on BBC's *Strictly Come Dancing*. I decided to put on a dance show with the help of Len's son, James Goodman, to raise funds for the charity. James and I wanted someone from *Strictly* to act as a judge as Len was away in America on the night of the event, and so he suggested Kristina because he said everybody on the show knew how much she loved children.

I was delighted at how readily Kristina accepted the invitation and very pleased that she agreed to stay for the dinner after the show. I started the charity because growing up near Dartford where Len had his dance school, I was forced to keep a terrible secret. Nobody knew that my father was extremely violent and my grandfather was a paedophile. Between the ages of three and seven I was exposed to extreme violence in my home and sexual abuse, which left me with learning difficulties at school. At charity events I always speak about my childhood and how dancing with Len helped to heal me and gave me the motivation to go on to become a newsreader and eventually start a charity to help protect children and give them a voice.

After my speech on that night I was surprised that Kristina asked to speak to me privately. Her eyes brimmed with tears as she explained that she had grown up in an environment where she was frightened all the time and did not feel loved. Like me, she felt that dancing had saved her and her dance school was the only place where she felt valued and safe.

Since that night, Kristina has put her heart and soul into helping me grow the charity and bring more children and more schools into the programme. In 2014, she took the decision to speak publicly about her childhood and has become the charity's patron. I imagine that many people who watch Kristina and believe her to have had a perfect and glamorous life will be shocked by the truth and how hard it has been for her to overcome the fear and loneliness of her childhood and become an international star.

Through the charity's learning programme, Kristina and I are now reaching thousands of children and helping them learn how to stay safe and how to value themselves.

One of the things I have come to learn in life is that the way to decide who your friends truly are is to look at their actions. In the last five years, Kristina has travelled all over the country meeting children and visiting schools talking about her childhood and how she overcame the challenges. One summer she even spent six weeks putting on a special dance programme for children in London's most deprived areas.

In 2014, I was honoured by *Best* magazine with their Bravest Women Award after Kristina nominated me for the work I do in raising awareness of child abuse and protecting children. It is pretty tough making yourself vulnerable and telling people about the parts of your life that were painful, but I believe that is the only way we will bring about change. The truth is it was very lonely for me on the stage until Kristina was by my side using all her courage to tell her own painful story. She has used all that wonderful passion and energy that can be seen in her dancing to bring greater awareness of the need to have a national education programme in our schools, which helps children protect themselves from danger and know how to ask for help.

I hope you will be as fascinated as I was to read the full story of Kristina's life because, as you will discover, it is very far from what you might think!

Sharon Evans, founder of Dot Com Children's Foundation

Introduction

What have you read about me in the papers? Or perhaps I should ask one important question first… Do you believe everything you read about me in the newspapers, magazines or internet articles?

Have you made up your mind about a person without ever actually knowing them or speaking to them, or hearing what they have to say?

I have been called a 'Siberian Siren', a 'man-eater', a 'vixen'; I am 'cold' and a 'predator'. I have been labelled a 'home-wrecker', a 'trouble-maker', a 'man-stealer'.

Apparently, I am at the 'centre of relationship breakdowns', I have a 'flirtatious nature' and I am now 'banned from dancing with married men'.

I sound like a pretty horrible person, don't I? But this book is my chance to tell you about the real me. I want to share with you the truth about all the press stories that have been written about me that would puncture the thickest-skinned person.

To this day I don't understand why there is so much media interest in me. I am just a dancer, a dancer who grew up in Russia. For me dancing wasn't just a hobby – it was my survival. I owe my existence to dancing. It made me strong; I showed it dedication and it rewarded me with determination. It was my one constant through a childhood of misery and darkness and it has now given me a career and a means to support my family. I have sacrificed relationships for it and I have celebrated success through it.

But my life wasn't always in the headlines and I wasn't always being judged on how I looked, whether I was dating this man or that man, whether I had broken up a marriage or a relationship. I have had adventures all over the world and I have met some amazing people in my life. Yes, I have made mistakes, and I admit those within these pages. But I have been a victim, too. I have had low points that have been spread across the pages of tabloids and I have had triumphs on the dance floor that don't get more than a passing mention in an occasional article.

But now it is time for you to read about the real me, right from the Russian's mouth. Here, my life is laid out in front of you and I hope after reading this book you will be able to see and understand the real me.

Lots of love,
Kristina

PROLOGUE

The Last Tango

The roar of the crowd was absolutely deafening. I had no idea the sound of 13,000 people cheering and stomping their feet would create such a mind-blowing noise. It felt like the O2 Arena had completely erupted.

Simon Webbe and I had just performed the last dance on the 2014 Strictly Come Dancing tour and we stood in the centre of the floor savouring every moment of that sweet sound. There was no sign of the standing ovation quietening down so we didn't move a muscle. We just held hands, with sweat dripping down our cheeks, our hearts hammering in our chests, looking up at the thousands of faces that were cheering us on. I felt completely overwhelmed.

'Remember this moment, this is why we worked so hard,' I whispered to him, although I don't think he heard a word I said over the noise of the audience.

This appreciation, it is a magic only dance can create. It has nothing to do with who you are, how you look or what you have been doing, it is simply a recognition of the two minutes of intense, powerful routine we had just performed. This was pure admiration for our dance and at one of the biggest venues in London; the emotion just drained out of me. It was a moment that I had dreamt about since I was a little girl first learning to dance in Russia. I needed that sort of approval then as much as I needed it now. As a dancer it is something you feed off, you crave it like a drug for without it all the hours of work, all the dedication, all the sacrifices you make are for nothing.

I was someone who probably yearned for it more than most. From about the age of six I had to seek attention and love from outside of my family. I had parents who were so intent on causing themselves misery and pain they ignored their only child, who was so desperate to be noticed. Dancing saved me more times than I can remember and it became my lifeline through the dark days of childhood and the tragedies of growing up in a country filled with crime and uncertainty. It took me to new places filled with promise and dreams and gave me opportunities I would never have thought possible. It also gave me the means to support my family and me and make those I love more comfortable.

And now, here I was, standing in the O2, listening to the most wonderful noise in the world. The dance we had just performed, the Argentine tango, was such a special dance for Simon and me: it was the last dance we performed on the previous series of the show and now we had come to the end of the road together. It was our last tango and it only got better when we were presented with the Glitterball trophy that night after winning the whole live tour. That was why we put so many hours into rehearsing; we had created this special relationship with the audience. To feel you have given them something that they enjoy is a feeling I can't describe, but I remember getting it from the very first competition I won when I was a little girl. If I couldn't get the approval from my mum and dad, I could get it from people watching me dance. So in a way, growing up with parents who hated each other made me the dancer I am today.

All children growing up in Soviet Russia had to have an after-school hobby; you were never idle or just hanging around. Whether it was music, gymnastics, dance… the pressure was to excel, to be the best to make your country proud. But for me dancing was more than just a way of passing the time and fitting in with social expectations: I did it to escape, I had to escape. Home was where there was fighting and arguing and hatred, and dancing took me away from all that.

I know there was a time when my parents were not fighting, though. To be fair to them, there was a time, before I was born, when they were happy. Young idealists with dreams and aspirations, they were living in a time when Russia was under Soviet rule and things were rigid, structured and you stuck to the rules. It was a time, way back in the seventies, when two people met and fell in love…

CHAPTER 1

Once upon a time in a land far away...

My parents were both students at the same Far Eastern polytechnic university in Vladivostok, Russia, when they met in 1976. Mum was studying shipbuilding and my dad wanted to become an engineer, and although it wasn't in the classroom of that college where they fell in love, it was at another typical student hangout – a party.

My mum, Larisa Osadchaya, was a lot more studious than my father, Igor Pshenichnykh, who was an aspiring musician and composer. He studied well enough to become an engineer but music was his real passion. He wrote several songs about Vladivostok, a port on the eastern coast of Russia; they are regularly played on the city's 'birthday', on 2 July each year. That day is called the 'day of the city' and we celebrate with parades and music. So although he isn't famous in the real world, as it were, his music and his songs about Vladivostok are fairly well

1

known there. My dad had a lovely voice; his music is perhaps classed as a mixture of pop and reggae, and he would write about the beauty of the city – the beaches and the sea and all of the little islands surrounding it. It is a beautiful place, a famous seaport in our country, and in the days of my parents studying and falling in love, it was, of course, part of the Soviet Union.

Vladivostok was a closed city, which meant that no one was allowed in without very specific travel papers authorised by the government. My mum told me later that you were allowed out of the city but coming into it was a different matter. You had to have special papers to travel into the city because of the naval base, the Soviet authorities being keen to protect and keep secret anything that was happening in Vladivostok. You might think that it was a strange profession for my mother to be in, the shipbuilding industry, but she was a highly educated, very intelligent young woman. She finished school with a gold medal – an accolade only the elite students received, and only very rarely in those days, for the Soviet Union education system was tough, and designed to push students to be the best.

Everything was a competition and the mantra was to win at everything you could, and for my mum, who loved to study and soak up everything she could, it was the perfect environment to nurture her love of learning. And shipbuilding appealed to her emotional side, as it seemed to her to be a very romantic ideal – to build ships in her country's largest port on the Pacific Ocean. She was an ideologist and wanted to do something big. Always reading, constantly studying, she was ever hungry to learn. I suppose part of her love of learning came from her own childhood, as her mother, my grandmother, Valentina Vorobieva, was a teacher. She taught what was then called 'household studies'. It was still being taught when I was in school and I think the best way to describe it is that boys learnt manly stuff – like how to bang a nail into a piece of wood, or something – and girls would learn how to knit or sew, or cook. It all sounds terribly old-fashioned now, I suppose, but that is what my grandmother taught in her school while my grandfather, Grigory Osadchy, was an engineer and also a highly educated man.

My mum's childhood wasn't a particularly happy one. When she was born on 5 January 1956, Grigory was well on his way to becoming an alcoholic; over the years it just got worse and he became a heavy drinker. Mum told me that when she was growing up quite often she would spend some nights staying awake, just waiting for my grandfather to get home drunk as he was very violent and would be physically aggressive towards my grandmother. When that happened, my grandmother would often take my mother away and they would end up sleeping overnight in the school where she taught, just to be safe for the night. And then in the morning, my mother would just wake up and walk along to her classroom and wait for the other students. Apparently my grandmother spent a lot of time struggling to keep the marriage together as divorce was frowned upon in those days, but because of all the violence and drinking, there wasn't really another option. My mum was twelve years old at the time, but she understood what it would mean for her mother to suffer the stigma of being 'a divorcee'. And despite the abuse my grandmother suffered, she would still rather that than have people know she was a divorcee.

My grandfather did eventually stop drinking. Not long after the divorce, he had some kind of seizure and was told by the doctors that if he didn't stop, he would be dead. After that, and after the divorce as well, I suppose he decided to change his ways completely. He quit his job as a high-level engineer and moved to a small village called Risovo, near a town called Arseniev, where his sister and some of his cousins lived, and there he completely turned his life around. Now he became a local hunter, a beekeeper and lived off the land, really, as a sort of farmer. He didn't make contact with my grandmother and my mother decided that she never wanted to hear from him either, although she did years later when I was nine years old and we went to visit him together – but more on that later.

My grandmother went on to marry a wonderful man, who became my mum's stepdad, and I class him as my grandad. His name was Boris Stolov and he was a geologist and went on lots of exciting expeditions. He was able to take my mum and grandmother around the country (the Soviet Union at that time would pay for family travel) and he absolutely cherished my grandmother. He loved my mother, too, and was very kind to her, helping with her education and supporting her decision when she finished school in 1973 to study engineering in Vladivostok.

Which is where, of course, at one of the hippy parties in the late seventies that my mum met my dad. He was singing and playing guitar with his band at this party and Mum has told me she instantly gravitated towards him. A good-looking guy with beautiful long black hair, he had a wonderful voice to boot and my mother, a good-looking woman herself, was instantly smitten. They began dating and it wasn't long afterwards that Mum fell pregnant. It was 1977 and she was twenty years old, and in Russia at that time, everything had to be done by the book. This meant that they had to get married fairly promptly as a child born out of wedlock was not the way things were done and so they registered an application to get married. This system is still used in Russia today: you have to apply to get married and then you are given a month by the court to organise your wedding. So that's what they did, and they married in a very small, intimate ceremony when my mum was three months' pregnant with me. As students, they received a small amount of money from the government for studying, and in those days there were initiatives in place whereby if you went into a local food shop and showed them that you were due to be married then you were granted extra food and could buy certain products at a discount.

The day before the wedding my grandparents from both sides – my grandmother and my 'new' grandfather Boris and my dad's mum Marina – all came to Vladivostok to see my parents get married. It wasn't a big wedding but Mum said it was fun because my dad and his bandmates played and sang. It is the Russian way, I believe, to make the best of everything. It doesn't matter if you don't have a lot, and at that time everyone was the same – it was all about having fun and making the best of a situation.

My parents had to move out of the accommodation they were in as students because once they married they weren't allowed to live in the student halls, so they had to find a flat to rent. Unfortunately, all the flats in the centre of Vladivostok, near the college, were really expensive so they had to move quite far out of the city in order to afford somewhere to live. An area on the outskirts was all that they could afford, and the flat they moved into was tiny. There was no furniture, no central heating and, due to a very dry summer causing the reservoir to dry up, there was no water either. This meant that my dad had to go out and fetch the water they needed so my mum could boil it and use it. He would have to walk for about twenty minutes each way, would carry the water back in two buckets, a trip he had to make three or four times a day. It was a tough time, and while I know my mum prepared for my arrival as well as she could, the only furniture they had was a big mattress on the floor and two chairs, which she put together for my crib.

I'll let her tell you in her own words about the day I came into the world…

It was a beautiful, sunny September day when I started going into labour with Kristina. It wasn't unusual for September to be a lovely warm month although to be honest, any thoughts of sunshine were quickly replaced by thoughts of pain when the labour began. It was 21 September and I called for a taxi to take me and Igor to the hospital. I was completely scared. I didn't know what would happen or what to expect and I just felt so young and helpless. I was in labour for nineteen hours with my daughter and I lost a lot of blood during that time. At no point was I offered any sort of painkillers and I desperately wanted to see my mother but she lived so far away.

Finally, after hours and hours of pain and exhaustion, on 22 September our daughter finally arrived in this world and it was all over. We were home two days later, back to our tiny little flat, and all I remember is that I cried the whole journey home. I was scared and I felt alone and I had a new baby to care for.

I understand now how hard it must have been for two young students, newly married with a baby. My mum had tried to read all the books that were available at the time about how to raise a child but with no relatives around to help and no money to buy anything, it was hard. She was breastfeeding me, so I was getting the nutrition I needed, but three weeks after I was born, my dad said enough was enough – they couldn't live like that any more. He gave my mum an ultimatum: either they sent me away to live with his mum in a city called Holmsk in Saxalin – which was three-hour flight from where we lived – or he would walk away. He couldn't deal with it any more and was ready to leave.

Mum was absolutely devastated. She was so scared that she would be left all on her own with a newborn that she made the heartbreaking decision to give me away…

CHAPTER 2

Pickling, preparing and performing

So my parents flew to Holmsk and gave me away to my dad's mother, Marina Pshenichnykh. She was a doctor but she wasn't practising at that time, she was working as a nurse at a kindergarten so she could take me into nursery and look after me there. And she had raised my dad alone after his real dad walked out on them.

I don't know what happened there really, only that the surname I use, Rihanoff, comes from my dad's father. To me it made sense to use the name Rihanoff. Some people say it is pronounced with an 'R', while others say it is with an 'L', Lihanoff. So why have I changed my name? In a sense I haven't, I am still Kristina Pshenichnykh – Rihanoff is my stage name. When I joined the *Dancing with the Stars* tour years later, they told me that no one would be able to pronounce Pshenichnykh properly and with twelve letters, it was a bit of a mouthful. So I adopted the stage name Rihanoff. Had my dad's father married my grandmother, she would have had the name Rihanoff, my father would then have had it and then my mother, when they married, would have used it. It made sense to me. As it was, Marina found herself another partner, a lovely man called Andrey. Everybody who knew him has told me that he would spend his days just carrying me in his arms all the time, and that to him I was his granddaughter. Unfortunately, he died from a heart attack before I was old enough to know him properly.

So that was my first year – mostly spent with my grandmother and Andrey while my mum went back to studying. But it was hard for her and she missed me. Although she tried to visit me, Holmsk was still a three-hour flight away. When I was nine months old she couldn't cope any longer and so she took me to stay with her mum and Boris, who lived slightly closer to her in a village called Kavalerovo. It meant that she could visit me more often and when she got her diploma and graduated with her degree in shipbuilding in 1979, she took me back properly to Vladivostok.

I was a year and five months old when she started working at the shipbuilding company so she would leave me with a babysitter, who was able to take me to the local kindergarten.

My mum's job was a big thing in Russia at that time. Every day when she left work, she would have her bag checked for documents, photos or sketches that she might have made of the ships or submarines. The Soviet Union was so secretive and didn't trust anyone, so it was a daily ritual for it to check nothing about its great navy was being leaked by an employee. The city had been closed for over thirty years due to it being the main marine base of the Soviet Pacific Fleet, but my parents never said it was a bad time for them. They both had a decent wage, more than doctors and teachers during Soviet Union times, and they also enjoyed lots of privileges from the professional unions. These included free travel and also free trips to 'health spas', which was where you could get checked over by a doctor and relax for a week. I did lots of those trips with my parents when I was a bit older and they were great fun.

You couldn't really complain about that, now could you?

The year my mum graduated and got her job was also the year my grandfather Boris was given a flat by the government because of his job as a geologist. That was very normal in the days of the Soviet Union: the government did provide for you and Boris was rewarded for his work and given a flat in Vladivostok. But he told them it needed to be a big flat as he had a big family, so they provided him with a large enough apartment for all six of us to live in – him, my grandmother, my mother, my father, me and my grandmother's other daughter, Valeria. My grandmother had her when she was forty-one years old so actually she is only a few years older than me and although she is technically my aunt and my mum's sister, I grew up thinking she was my sister.

We grew up together and went to the same school, with Valeria taking me to my classes. People would say, 'Oh, you are an only child, poor you!' but I grew up with her like a sister. She would walk me to school, we would gossip and play together, fight constantly and generally act like siblings; we were so close. Every New Year's Eve we would put on a show for my parents and grandparents and make them sit down and watch us. It was a tradition and my aunt and I loved to perform for them. We would act out a Russian fairytale and I would be the princess and she would often be the evil queen. And then when they had all gone to bed we would sneak out of our rooms to peek at our presents under the New Year's tree.

I loved living as a big family under one roof – it was a typical arrangement for families in Russia at that time – and I was very happy. There were three rooms and up until I was five years old I stayed in my parents' room with them, then I moved in with Valeria. My grandmother and Boris slept in the sitting room as it was the largest room.

It was one of the happiest times of my childhood and I felt loved and cared for by everyone. My grandmother was the kindest woman you could ever meet, always on my side. I think I was quite a rebellious child but she would always stick up for me.

Unfortunately, my parents had quite a turbulent relationship. They were both young and didn't really know what to do and what *not* to do in front of me. They knew I was always being looked after by my grandparents so it gave them a bit of freedom to go out a lot and party, knowing I was home and that I would be looked after and fed and put to bed.

The biggest problem was that my dad was always caught up in his music and perhaps the idea of family wasn't something he put a lot of thought into. He grew up as an only child raised by a single mum and she was always telling him what a wonderful musician he could be. I think, although it is natural for a mother to encourage a child, constantly telling him that he could be famous musician and a world-famous composer filled his head with a lot of dreams. His music was also influenced by her, as she had gone to Cuba in the 1960s – it was a country that had a very strong relationship with Russia. I remember my grandmother telling me about her memories of Cuba: she said that nobody ever seemed to work, they just sang and danced outside all day long! She couldn't understand how they could survive because they just seemed to be out dancing on the streets all day. It also meant that my dad was influenced a lot by that laid-back lifestyle, and in his music by Cuban songs. There was no Beatles music or anything else in Soviet Russia back then – you weren't allowed to play foreign music on the radio because it was considered propaganda so the only sort of foreign songs that could be played were Cuban. Dad once told me that he and his friends would sneak into one of his mate's garages and secretly listen to *Voice of America*. They would take in dictionaries and try to translate the words in the songs without being caught.

One of my earliest memories was when I must have been about three years old, dancing to Cuban music performed by my dad. And that was when I started to dance. At the house I was always dancing in front of my parents while my dad would play with ten of his mates, who would all have different instruments. He studied guitar at the local music school near where he grew up and had a real love and passion for music and singing from a young age. I think I have definitely inherited a love of song, dance and performance from him. His music was his first love and eventually I suppose that is what broke up his relationship with my mother: he put music in front of everything else.

To begin with, I didn't really understand what the arguments were about. I was a daddy's girl and if ever he was playing for a local music festival or a wedding – and he played at lots of weddings – my mum would take me and I would go and dance in front of everyone and in front of him on stage. To me he was my big star – there was my dad, playing on a stage! And the best thing was that he would sometimes take me up onto the stage too, which is where I may have got my love of performing. *Lights, camera, action!* I felt connected with him on that level, whereas my mum was always the strict one, the one making me do my homework or clean the flat. She was the one who would yell at me if I failed to do something on time – she was a very organised sort of woman and there wasn't a lot of wiggle room with her. It was perhaps why I saw Dad as more of a friend and ally; I just wanted to spend time with him, dancing and listening to him sing. But of course it was a selfish way to live. He would think about his music and his band to such an extent that there wasn't much left for him to give my mum or me.

It was a terrible marriage – my parents were always fighting, shouting and yelling at each other. My grandmother and grandfather were always there and able to take care of me so in a way, if it was making me sad or upset, at least I had them. I remember there were times when my dad would leave for a couple of weeks and not come home at all. He would just go and nobody would know where he had gone and then all of a sudden he would reappear and the fighting would start again. He was constantly going, coming home and then leaving again. I later found out he was with his mates and playing his music and that was all he cared about; he wasn't putting a lot of effort into building a relationship with me.

But I was young and so whom did I blame? My mum, of course. She was the strict one, the one making me clean or read, or do boring stuff. I blamed her for the fact that my dad was leaving the house for weeks on end, when I just wanted him to be around. In my childish mind, I blamed her when he wasn't there. The problem was they were both very strong-minded people who wanted certain things in life. Dad, especially, may not have envisaged that he would be married so young and have a child, when all he wanted to be was a famous musician. He might have felt in some kind of way that he had been robbed of that chance.

*****

There are perhaps many people who didn't live in Soviet Russia during the early 1980s who believe that it was a very grim and terrible place and time. But actually my mum said life was very stable there. It was guaranteed you would have a paycheck at the end of the month, you would have your medical treatments for free, education was free and you got your accommodation, all of which were granted to you by the places at which you worked. You didn't have to worry, it was all very stable; nobody lived feeling scared of tomorrow.

But there were some restrictions. We had vouchers for certain foods, like meat and poultry, and you only received a certain number of kilograms of meat per person per week. It meant that when you went to the shop to get the meat, the whole family had to queue to make sure that you got the most you could – the most to which you were entitled as a family. Sometimes the queues were quite long, especially before big holidays like Christmas and New Year. On those occasions we always went along as a family to queue and take the meat home. We would make all this delicious food, like pelmeni, which are Russian-style dumplings with meat inside. You could freeze them and then eat them after a big holiday and they would be so filling! That is why everyone stayed in line for the meat – all six of us – because it wasn't just about eating, it was the tradition of preparing the meat, storing it and getting the most out of every scrap.

Of course, sometimes the queues would be long and it would be very boring to wait there – not much fun, especially for a child! Some shops would put up signs announcing something like the meat would go on sale at 5pm, so people would come and line up earlier to be first so that when the time came, the line would be huge! But you couldn't do anything else; just wait.

There was a lot of canned food available, and given that we lived by the sea, I remember there was always plenty of tinned seaweed in our flat. It was almost a staple meal: we had lots of seaweed salads as my mum would buy cans and cans of the stuff and she would always be making it into salads to feed to me during the winter. She told me it was good for me (and it wasn't as bad as it sounds, I promise).

The local agriculture system was good as we had lots of fruit and vegetables from the farms in the summer but in winter, as a family, we always made plenty of pickled foods. Pickling was one of my mum and grandmother's specialities. They had special recipes to make the sauce and they would literally pickle everything in it – cucumbers, tomatoes, parsnips and peppers and all sorts of other foods, so that in winter, when there wasn't fresh stuff available, we were still able to have fruit and vegetables.

My grandmother and Grandfather Boris had a little summer house about an hour away by train from where we lived, where they would grow a lot of vegetables too and I would spend much time there in the summer. We would catch the train out of Vladivostok to the summer house to look after what was growing there or to plant new things for the season. We had all the berries – including strawberries and blueberries – and of course, tomatoes and cucumbers and potatoes, too. Basically, we grew everything, and then we would gather it to store at home on the balcony of our flat for winter time. So fruit and vegetables would be pickled and my mother and grandmother would also make marmalade for winter. It was our way of surviving: we prepared for winter in the summer and everything was made from scratch.

Cheese was another product that was limited by the state to a weight in kilograms per person so again, you had to queue for it, but it was available. And we love cottage cheese in Russia – I remember eating lots and lots of it! I suppose the only noticeable thing about food in Soviet Russia at that time was there wasn't much variety. But it didn't matter; everyone had food all year round because we made sure we prepared and stored it properly. In fact, rather than being short on food, the complete opposite was true – our tables were always so full of food, and after big holidays we would eat leftovers for more than a week. Nothing was ever wasted – we used everything, and it was all cooked from scratch and either eaten or preserved. Cooking was a big tradition, too: my mother and grandmother learnt how to do the pickling and preserving when they were young. In school, during the lessons in 'household studies' where the boys and girls would be separated, the girls would learn cookery skills and how to prepare food for winter.

When it came to food, trade was limited to between the fifteen Soviet States but I suppose it did still give us a taste of the 'exotic'. Ukraine candies were amazing, we loved them so, *so* much and because Vladivostok was a seaport, we were able to provide the whole of Russia with fish. Tinned caviar, for example, which everyone eats in Russia, was so common a food we ate it all the time. I remember red caviar in particular – we would have lots on special occasions like Christmas or New Year. It seems to be such a delicacy over here, and so expensive too! And I remember the finest chocolate came from Moscow – that was the best kind. There was one brand called Mishka Kosolapy, which had hazelnuts in it and I loved it. It was the biggest treat ever to have some of that.

The elderly were particularly taken care of by the Soviet Union. There were shops called 'Veteran', which were purely for veterans of war and their families. Certain coupons would be given to them to get special foods, or foods at a cheaper price. The pensioners and veterans were looked after so well and that is why, if you ever spoke to an older person who had lived through Soviet Union times and asked them why they didn't hate the system, they would never say that they did – why would they, when they had such stability and were so well looked after? Of course, in just a few years' time, it was all to change.

CHAPTER 3

Dancing with boys

I remember being in kindergarten when I was five years old and there would be a woman who would come in and teach us folk dancing. Other days she would teach us disco dancing and I absolutely loved it. I couldn't wait for her to come to visit us. Shortly after that, I started school, even though I was only six years old and normally, in the Soviet Union then, everyone started when they were seven. But because I was born in September and my mum persuaded them that I was very capable and would study hard, I began school early. And it was in First Grade that I found out that the woman who had visited our kindergarten was a scout and she was looking for local children to join her dance school. Best of all, she wanted me! She wrote to my parents to say that she was opening a ballroom dance school and that she had seen me dance at kindergarten and would like me to come along.

My parents and I went to see it, I had a few lessons and the woman told them that I had considerable potential; she could see a lot of talent and she would like to offer me a place. She also told them that she already had a dance partner in mind for me, as you always have to have a partner in competitive ballroom dancing, which made me think she must really want me to join. And that is where my journey into dance really began. It was so exciting and I was so pleased to be doing an after-school activity that I absolutely loved; I couldn't wait to finish school each day and go to dance classes.

After-school activities were heavily encouraged in the Soviet Union – Heaven forbid that a child should be on the streets doing nothing! Whether it was ballet, gymnastics, music or art school, you had to be doing something, and you were always encouraged to strive for excellence and not be idle. So we were all groomed to do something as an after-school activity, and mine was dancing.

I would go three days a week and sometimes the whole family would come with me and watch me perform. I loved it. I just wanted to dance. My first dance partner was a sweet boy called Roman, a very talented, very handsome boy. He was seven years old and my parents became quite friendly with his parents too, as we spent a lot of time rehearsing together. But his father was quite a senior officer in the army and when Roman was ten, he made him stop dancing as he wanted him to go into the army, too. It was a shame, because we had such fun together, and we took part in our very first dance competition together. I remember it so well. My mum made my dress, spending all night sewing it from whatever material she could find. She stitched feathers on the hem and I couldn't wait to put it on and have my hair curled. It wasn't even an important competition, for it was just among the other children at the dance school, so pretty low-key in reality, but for me it was so exciting. And we won it. I was over the moon! I had no fear of competing, no nerves whatsoever, and I think that is when my parents knew that dance would be good for me as a child: they didn't have to force me to go, and they didn't need to worry about what I would be doing after school.

So what was it like performing at six years old and dancing with – oh, my goodness – a boy? I don't know, when people ask me about children dancing together so young, what is so odd – it was just natural. Boys and girls just danced; there was no shyness, no embarrassment. The truth is that ballroom dancing is brilliant for children; you learn how to communicate with each other freely and you don't feel silly at all. I loved dancing with Roman and we had good fun together.

I couldn't get enough of ballroom dancing. Having performed in front of an audience once, that was it – I was out performing whenever I could. I had no fear. It was such an adrenaline rush going out on stage in front of everyone and the school were very proud of having children who could perform, and perform well. It was such a strong ideology that was constantly being drummed into us: if you were going to do something you had to be the best. And in the beginning, when I was six, seven and eight years old, nothing was a struggle. It was very easy for me to pick up the moves. I had a natural rhythm and could dance easily to the music. As I grew older, however, I found that dancing became a lot more about technique, and that you really had to work hard if you wanted to progress.

Ballroom dancing at that time was like an awakening giant;

21

suddenly it was everywhere, its popularity growing in every city and town. It was good because it meant that the competitions were springing up all over the place and you could take part in so many. I remember going to one competition, which was a two-hour drive away; it was being held at a dance school considered to be one of the best in the area. But Roman and I didn't even make it to the final. I was heartbroken. At nine years old I thought my life was over, that is how devastated I was. It's funny thinking about that now – it must have been the first time that I realised that you can't win everything. But it did make me even more determined.

At home, my parents' relationship was getting worse. It became normal for my dad to go away for a couple of weeks at a time and we wouldn't hear anything from him. We got used to it. I remember being rude to my mum and telling her I hated her because it was all her fault Dad had left again. I completely blamed her for him going, and even though I didn't know what the arguments were about (and usually they were about him wanting to play music and not to be in a house with six other people and have to behave responsibly), I used to blame my mum.

Everyone was under pressure to be good role models in every way. It was what was expected of us in society, and was drummed into people – to work hard, to be the best – so I think for my dad, even though he would go away and perform and have a break where he could concentrate on his music, eventually he'd still have to come back and work. He had to be a grown-up. Whereas my mum, a very opinionated, very intelligent person, always she tried to be the best and to set a good example. She never spoke about how bad her childhood had been, growing up with a drunken father who would beat her mother, she just tried to work as hard as she could and strived to be the best. So I think when her own marriage was falling apart that added to the sadness and disappointment she already felt about family life. She knew how bad her marriage was. The only thing really gluing our family together at the time was my grandparents, and especially my grandmother. She was always trying to bring us all together as a family, constantly trying to get us to spend days together.

There were times when they were good together, my mum and dad, and they would keep up appearances and both come to my school for certain special days. But I knew how bad it was; there was no escape from all the arguing and fighting.

Actually, there *was* an escape: dance school. Although to get to dance classes in the afternoons, there was the small matter of going to school first. My mum would wake me up every morning before she went to work to braid my hair because you always had to have your hair tied back so it was neat and tidy. You weren't allowed to wear it down so Mum would wake me really early, at 6am, to braid my hair then I would go back to sleep for a bit and she would go to work. The boys had to have their hair cut short and cropped so from a young age we were disciplined to look good and be well groomed. When you are a child, it suits you and you just accept that is the way it is.

I think when you get older you want to express yourself more and be different and that is where it can be more difficult, I suppose, when you develop your own style. But at school, everyone was striving to work hard and be the best, no one was judging you by what you wore, everyone was the same. For our

23

school uniform we had little dark brown or black dresses and we had to wear white lace collars and white wrist cuffs, too. The cuffs and collars were removable so you could take them off each week, wash them and then sew them back in. Boys wore short jackets and white shirts and trousers, and we all had a feeling of being the same. There was no judging how we looked because we all looked identical – the same uniform, the same shoes, the same bag for everyone.

But the teachers could dress how they wished. I remember having an obsession with my history teacher, who was a young woman who always looked so glamorous. She was always dressed beautifully and looked amazing with her make-up, which was something that was completely forbidden for us young girls. We weren't allowed to go near it or wear it at all. In my dancing world I had a little taste of make-up with a bit of glitter around my eyes or some lip gloss, but in school it was totally forbidden. You would be put up in front of the class and shamed about why young girls shouldn't wear make-up if you dared put any on.

School would begin every year on 1 September. The education system in Soviet Russia was something the government took a lot of pride in. There was a very strong, solid system, everything had an order and there was no room for disobedience or misbehaviour. The schools were kept very clean and very neat; everything was in order. In every hallway there were pictures of Lenin, Stalin and Brezhnev next to a red Soviet Union flag and every Monday morning each class had to line up in the corridor and the best student that week would be called out and their achievements celebrated with the whole school. It was such an honour to be congratulated like that – you really wanted to be that person.

For the first three grades we were taught by one teacher and then from fourth grade upwards there were different teachers for different subjects. My teacher in the first three grades was extremely strict. She was known as the best at the school for the newcomers, for those in Grades 1–3, and every parent wanted their child to be in her class. I think the only reason I was put in her class was because my aunt, Valeria, who was already in the fifth grade, had an English teacher who was a good friend of my grandmother. The English teacher put in a good word for me so I could get into that class, which was brilliant.

I knew the teacher I had was the best. An older lady, she was very strict and had won all sorts of teaching prizes. She had been at the school for ever, or so it seemed. We were all petrified of her!

CHAPTER 4

School, Stalin
and sick notes

Our classroom had three desks to a row and about five rows in total, and we sat in pairs at each desk. At the front was a portrait of Lenin on the wall and a big map of the Soviet Union and its neighbouring republics. There were never any other maps of any other countries: it was just the Soviet Union that mattered. After the third grade, when you would have a specific geography classroom, I think there might have been other maps showing other countries, but in the first three grades it was just the Soviet Union.

I was seated at the front and I hated it. The less able pupils would be made to sit at the back but I didn't appreciate that there was a difference, really. It was what it was: you didn't question it when you were told where to sit. I was told I had to sit next to this little boy on the front row because he had told his mum he liked me. Boys and girls had to sit together

27

to begin with, but I didn't like that at all. I just wanted to sit with other girls but I had to sit with this boy called Maxim, whose mum was working on the local TV station at the time. She was the local star and we all loved her. Apparently Maxim really liked me and he told his mum he didn't want to sit with anyone but me. She told the teacher and then she asked my parents if I would mind sitting with Maxim – and because she was a local celebrity of course my parents and the teacher didn't argue.

I didn't want to sit at the front at all because I hated to be right by the teacher's desk but Maxim's mum wanted him to be at the front and therefore I would have to sit there, too. So I cried a lot! I absolutely did not want to sit at the front near the teacher – I just felt so self-conscious. Not that I could really complain either; you were told what to do and you were raised to respect anyone in authority. You never spoke back to your teacher and if you ever dared to answer back then you were put in front of the whole school, told what a bad person you were and made an example of in front of everyone. You couldn't be different either. There was a boy in our class who was left-handed and our teacher really pushed him and made him do extra lessons to make him right-handed. They put a lot of effort into that, I remember.

I was dyslexic, although I wasn't diagnosed until years later, and I found some subjects easier than others. My mum was always making me do extra reading and learning at home so I had excellent grades because she was spending so much time with me and helping me to go through my homework. She wanted to push me as well as encourage me. In a sense, we were all under pressure to be good pupils and get good grades. If you weren't getting good marks then your parents would be told and they would be questioned to see if there was a problem at home or if they weren't encouraging you to spend enough time on homework. So it all had a knock-on effect and it was embarrassing if you didn't get good grades; we were scared to fail.

There was a system of competition amongst everyone to be the best so the classes competed against each other, too. Whichever class was getting the best results reflected on your teacher, which in turn reflected on the school. So in the system you had to be good for your school, for your neighbourhood, for your city and for your country. It was the ideology in Russia at that time to be the best of the best; it was drummed into us. And I had a lot of pressure from my mum, who was a gold medallist from her school and would always be going on at me to study. But at the same time we all had to conform and be the same, so it was a bit confusing really.

Whenever there was a big public holiday or we had a day for our army, for example, we all had to wear red square ties with our school uniform and we were called the 'pioneers' of Lenin's party. I was so proud! I was so excited as it was a big deal and we were presented with our red ties by the school and the teachers would put them around our necks. We would then have to salute and say something in praise of Lenin and Stalin and the Communist Party. We had an oath we had to recite, too:

I, Pshenichnykh, Kristina, having now joined the ranks
of the Vladimir Lenin All-Union Pioneer Organisation,
in the presence of my comrades solemnly promise: to

passionately love my fatherland and to cherish it as I can, to live, study and fight as the Great Lenin has instructed, as the Communist Party teaches me, and as such to always carry out the laws of the Pioneers of the Soviet Union.

I was so proud to come home with the red tie around my neck, I felt so grown-up. When you were older, say, from fifteen or sixteen years old, you would progress to being a 'Komsomol' of Lenin's party, which was the youth division of the Communist Party of the Soviet Union. A lot of adults would be in the Party and you would wear a badge. It was a very prestigious thing, something to be proud of, and you became part of it at school – it was just a natural part of growing up (my mum and dad were both in Komsomols at school). It also meant that we would parade in the big square courtyard at the front of the school. There would be a speech from one of the teachers and one of the pupils who had been recognised for a particular achievement would also give a speech. This would be about the Socialist Party and how proud we were to be a part of it. We would then salute a picture of Lenin at the end of the parade. You don't question anything as a child – you are brought up in it, and you want to belong to that big Party and make others around you proud, which is why there was such an emphasis on doing well and being the best. You wanted to fit in and not let anyone down.

Back then in the Soviet Union it was ingrained in you from the word go to have respect for your elders: you would never speak back to your teacher or an older person. We were all quite well-behaved kids. Heaven forbid you ever did misbehave at school as you would be put in front of the whole school and shamed about what you had done. And then you would be sent home to tell your parents what had happened, which was the worst thing in the world. It happened to me once: I was in third grade and must have been about eight or nine years old. It was then that my mum decided she wanted to make contact with her real dad. My grandmother never wanted to have anything more to do with him but I think my mother was ready to meet him again to see if she could have a relationship with him. She wrote to some relatives and somehow they found his address in the little village that he lived in. They exchanged letters for a while before he asked my mum to his village to visit him. We went with her, my dad and me, and as it was a long way away – we had to catch an overnight train, a bus and then another bus – she decided to go for a long weekend to make the most of it.

So my mum wrote a note to my teacher to ask if it was OK for me to skip school on Friday and Saturday (it was only a short day on Saturday) but my teacher said no. I told you she was strict! But I really wanted to go with my parents and so I told them she had said yes. So I lied to my parents and we all went and I remember going back to school on the Monday and my teacher asked me where I had been. I thought it would be fine if I just said I was sick or something but of course she then wanted a note from my mother to say I had been ill. So I lied again and said I had forgotten it and this went on for a couple of days until she rang my mother at work. Then things got bad, really, really bad. They both found out that I had lied and I had my mum and dad yelling and screaming at me and then my teacher shaming me in front of the whole school, telling them that I had lied and done a terrible thing.

But you know what? It was worth it, even though nobody was nice to me for a couple of days. As I was only a child and too young to be told of the history between my grandfather and my grandmother, it was just a cool trip with my parents to visit this new grandad whom I hadn't even known existed. He had a big house with lots of animals – dogs, cats, birds, chickens and roosters running around. And he also had a bunch of beehives and would let me taste this really fresh honey, which was wonderful. I didn't know at the time what it meant for my mum to go and visit her dad. She didn't tell my grandmother where we all went because she knew she would be upset, but I remember she found out a couple of years later and then I understood the truth about what had happened when my mother was young.

I was ten years old and I heard my mother and grandmother talking in raised voices about it. My grandmother had somehow found out that my mother had visited her real dad and she was very, very upset. She couldn't understand why my mother would want to see him and she reminded Mum about all the times he would hit her and how they had gone to stay at the school to escape him. Also, she didn't understand how my mother could forgive him, although in her defence, I think it is human nature to try to understand where you come from. My grandfather had stopped drinking by then and my mum explained to my grandmother how he was a different man now and that he had changed his lifestyle and was taking better care of himself. He had told my mother that my grandmother was the love of his life and he would never be able to forgive himself for treating her the way he had.

Grandad had never remarried; he just lived on his own

with his animals and never formed any other relationships. A strong man, he was also very clever and matter-of-fact and had been in the army, too. I certainly think my mother got her personality from him rather than my grandmother, who was a very soft woman. My mother was very definite in her decisions, something I think she got from him.

And there wasn't really anything soft about my mother either. As well as the constant fighting with my dad, I felt that she would never just talk to me either – she always seemed to shout! I understand now, although I didn't then, how frustrated she must have been with my dad and the state of their marriage. She would shout at me constantly, almost taking her anger out on me. Very full-on, she was also very strict with me. I might have tried to say something back to her once or twice but then I would get a smack and so I would never do it again.

As I have said, you would never disrespect your elders, ever, and so we did grow up with a lot of appreciation for older people. When I was ten or eleven years old there was a school programme that involved us going to visit war veterans and helping them in any way you could. I used to visit a lady, a war veteran who lived alone – she was so sweet. I would wash the floors for her, clean her kitchen and go to the shop and fetch her some vegetables and other things. Her family couldn't visit her every day as they lived outside Vladivostok, but the government knew where the elderly veterans lived and those who were living alone and at their most vulnerable. They would then be reported to the local schools so the students could help. It was a really considerate scheme and we felt we were doing a good thing. It did teach us to be compassionate and to show respect for our elders, especially those who had been through so much. And so it became second nature to help them whenever we could – even if that meant just helping someone to cross the street or giving them a seat on public transport.

CHAPTER 5

Wanting to be a Masha

After the third grade, you moved classrooms and had different teachers for each subject. It meant you could sit where you wanted – which was wonderful for me as I had been made to sit next to Maxim all that time. Now I was able to sit with my friend, Vera, whom I knew from outside school as we lived in the same apartment block.

We would quite often play together, but she was also a very studious girl. She would always get straight As in all of the subjects and I wanted to be just like her. I did study quite well and really loved subjects like History, Literature and Russian Language, but I hated Maths, Algebra and Physics – not my thing at all. From the fourth grade upwards school became even more strict and intense. There was lots of homework and everyone had the same subjects to study until they left school. Nowadays you can specialise in certain subjects if they are going to be subjects you want to study in more depth and graduate in from college, but when I was at school there was a big emphasis on everyone studying exactly the same thing, which was very demanding.

I remember we all loved English lessons – although I used to think it was a little pointless and I couldn't understand why I would ever need to learn English. So I wasn't that keen on it to begin with, and when our class was split into two groups to study it, I was pleased to have a teacher who spent most of the time doing her nails and didn't make us learn a lot, whereas the other group had a very strict teacher. Ours would give us a paragraph to translate and that would be it for the whole lesson. We thought we were very lucky until one week she was sick and they merged the two groups. It was only then that we realised we knew absolutely nothing compared to the other group. The teacher only spoke in English, and we realised we hadn't learned anything.

I wasn't a lonely child at school but I could probably only count Vera as my friend. It didn't help that I felt like an outsider because of my name, which I hated. I was the only girl in school with the name Kristina, and I was so cross with my mum.

'Why did you give me that name? Everyone makes fun of me with that stupid name! I want a different name!' I would shout at her. And she would say, 'OK, what name would you want? Something like Masha? Do you want to be like everyone else?'

I was also so caught up with my dancing that I just never really wanted to play with anyone after school because I always wanted to go to dance classes. Dance school was where I made friends and had lots of friends, boys and girls, as we all shared a common interest. For me it was a happy place, and fun to be among my friends. Even though I loved living with my grandparents and my aunt, my parents were still fighting all the time. And Dad was constantly leaving home and coming back and I just kept blaming my mum. Dance school was my escape and I especially loved going away on trips to take part in competitions. I was never homesick. No one at dance school knew what my home life was like so in a way I felt free – I could be myself and I was praised and appreciated because I was good at dancing.

Don't get me wrong, it was never praise that wasn't earned; we definitely had to prove ourselves to be good dancers and hard workers to warrant any admiration, so it felt good to be doing something well. It was a happy place for me and I definitely loved performing on the stage because it was a place where I too felt loved and appreciated. I was somebody worthy of attention on stage whereas at home, probably from the age of nine or ten, I wasn't getting a lot of attention from my parents – my dad especially. Maybe that sounds harsh. I guess to a certain extent I did have my parents' attention as they always supported me in dance competitions and made an effort on my birthday but to me, I think I felt a lack of attention from them as parents. My mum tried her best to make up for my dad's absences when she would take me to see the ballet, theatre shows and the circus. She really broadened my horizons, taking me to see some amazing shows that captured my imagination. I was a huge animal lover when I was young and cats were my favourite – I loved them! So when the cats' circus came to the city she would take me as a treat, as well as a way to compensate for my father being away.

When he was at home it was a lot worse as they were so

caught up in their own problems I felt rejected a lot of the time, or that I was in the way. I certainly don't think they cared much about me as they would always fight in front of me, and they would be so aggressive with each other. Can you imagine how awful it is to see your parents so angry towards each other? And they wouldn't hold anything back; they wouldn't try to hide their arguments. I was a constant witness to the shouting and screaming and it upset me a lot. I did cry quite often, but that was worse as they would then take their anger out on me and start shouting at me, too. My grandmother tried to calm them down and stop them from yelling, but there wasn't much chance of escape in our three-room flat.

The only bonus of living with six people in a smaller flat was that you didn't need to worry about the heating quite so much in winter. There was a lot of body heat generated so sometimes the central heating didn't have to be on full blast, which in Russia, during winter time, is the only way to survive. Our winters are extremely cold and temperatures can sometimes drop to -20°C. It was also very windy, for we were right on the coast so the wind chill from the sea can sometimes make it feel like -40. And I hate the cold!

I really didn't like the winters at all but the one good thing was that there was always plenty of snow, really deep, thick snow, which meant that snowball fights were part of daily life and my aunt and I would have great fun travelling to and from school on our sleighs. It does make me laugh how in the UK things come to a halt at the first sign of a snowflake. I can't imagine how people here would cope with the snow we used to get in Russia. We had so much, but it was never a problem because people were used to it. Schools would always be open and people had snow chains on the wheels of their cars so there were no transport difficulties either. Always we had to be prepared for snow, and we were.

In the summer the temperatures could get very high. It would reach 30°C in August, which was fine but it was also 98 per cent humidity too: humid and hot. We would spend lots of time outdoors, often by the sea in summer camp. My mum would get free vouchers for summer camp from work and I loved it. In Russia, in Soviet Union times, the schools would always break up in early June and then you would have June, July and August to enjoy summer before going back to school on 1 September. My dance school often held a few competitions in June (there was usually a big one at the beginning of July) and then after that we were released on holiday. I loved summer camp – there were always so many activities to do and always some kind of dancing which, of course, I loved. It was fun meeting new people and I enjoyed the company and being away from home. I always went with my aunt, who being older had already started dating boys so she loved it because it gave her the freedom to see them, and I loved it because I was able to dance and perform. And just being away from home was fun.

Summer camp, as well as being fun and a great place to learn and take part in new activities, was also fairly health-orientated, too. I suppose in a way the Soviet Union wanted to reinforce the notion of us being a strong, healthy generation and so every morning at camp we would have to stand in front of a quartz lamp to get our daily dose of vitamin D. It was something that was done across the whole of Russia – I didn't think much about it, I just lived it. I took my place in the Soviet system, although it was a system of contradictions, too. On the one hand there was a lot of pressure on Russia in the big sporting events, like the Olympics, to be the best and to win every event. But at the same time you had to conform and be equal with everyone else as well. My aunt was very sporty, and would often represent the school at athletic events; the whole family was very proud of her. I loved it when I was old enough to move out of my parents' room and in with her. There was a little desk where we could study but mostly we would just spend time together, chatting and gossiping. Before 6pm I was allowed in the living room and I could watch a couple of hours of children's TV on our big old chunky black-and-white television set.

Not that I really had much time to watch TV, what with dancing and Mum making sure I was doing my homework and studies. When she wasn't arguing with my dad, she always made sure I was working as hard as I could. As well as being a very clever woman herself, Mum was also extremely good-looking. She was so beautiful – we would walk out of our apartment building and she would have men turning their heads to watch her. It was embarrassing as a kid and I remember saying to her, 'Mum, every man is looking at you!'

Because she was also very outgoing, she had lots of friends. Whenever she took me out with her, she always made sure we were both dressed up and looking our best. She would make me wear a big bow on my head too, made from her red polka-dot scarf. She'd tie it into a bow and put it on my hair and sometimes it was bigger than my head! But she wanted me to look beautiful and she would sew some wonderful outfits for me. She always got a lot of attention from men and yes, that was probably hard for my dad to see as well, but she really couldn't help it. Sociable and intelligent, she was able to strike up a conversation with anyone and had no shortage of admirers. It probably led to quite a few arguments with Dad. As well as his regular disappearances, the fights were getting worse and worse.

Little did I realise, though, that living with my grandmother, Boris and my aunt would actually turn out to be one of the happiest times of my childhood – at least other people were around for me to talk to. But those living arrangements were not to last. In 1988, my dad was given a flat with his work. I would have been eleven years old around then and in 1989, my parents and I moved out of the big flat that we had shared with my grandparents and aunt and into our own little flat.

That was when my life started to get really tough.

CHAPTER 6

There may be trouble ahead. But while there's moonlight and music...

The year my parents and I moved into the new flat given to my dad by the government was also the year when my country, as I had known it so far, changed beyond all recognition. Not only did this change affect the whole country, it brought about a change in my own life too, marking it as the time when my life and my country simultaneously began to fall apart.

In a way Dad was quite lucky that he got the flat from his work before everything started closing down. He actually lost his job a short while after we moved into our new home, for it was a time when companies closed and people stopped getting paid by the government. My mum was still going to work at the shipbuilding company but she hadn't been paid for a long, long time and eventually she had to leave her job, too. The whole country turned wild, in a sense. Mum said it was like we were at war, just without the bombs. That was how it felt: we were living in a war zone, everything was uncertain, no one knew what would happen. It was the start of Perestroika, and to give you some idea of what was happening, I will let the history books explain:

In 1989, Soviet leader Mikhail Gorbachev decided to implement the policies of Perestroika, an economic 'restructuring'. It is often considered that this movement was the cause of the dissolution of the Soviet Union in 1991. Over the course of 1990–1, 15 countries declared their independence from the Soviet Union (Armenia, Azerbaijan, Belarus, Estonia, Georgia, Kazakhstan, Kyrgyzstan, Latvia, Lithuania, Moldova, Russia, Tajikistan, Turkmenistan, Ukraine and Uzbekistan) and the adoption of varying forms of market-economy in those post-Communist States, together with the rise of business oligarchs, led to a general decline in living standards. Rich Russian business entrepreneurs emerged under Gorbachev and by the end of the Soviet era and during Perestroika, many Russian businessmen imported or smuggled goods into the country and sold them, often on the black market, for a hefty profit. They became well-connected entrepreneurs to the corrupt, elected Russian government and they became extremely unpopular with the Russian public. Gang crime increased as the rich and poor divide became apparent. The businessmen and the gangs that were enforcing their rule are commonly thought to be the cause of much of the turmoil that plagued Russia following the collapse of the Soviet Union.

Our new flat was in a new development area in Vladivostok so nothing had been established yet – there weren't even any trees around. We had a couple of bad winters when we had no heating at all – during Perestroika everything just seemed to stop working. The new flat was quite a way from where we used to live – in reality only about half an hour on public transport but it felt far enough away for me. The move also meant I had to change schools and make new friends, which was pretty tough, but the worst thing of all was that there was no dance school in the area so I didn't dance for about a year.

For a twelve-year-old who loved to dance this was a very hard time indeed and now, of course, I was living in a flat with just my parents. There were no grandparents around to try and calm them down and the fighting became unbearable. They would argue non-stop, day and night, and it was absolutely horrific because there were just no boundaries. Sometimes it was physical, and a book or something else would be thrown, accompanied all the while by yelling and screaming. They would just fight and fight and fight. Dad had no money as he had lost his job and the money he would earn from his music gigs he wouldn't bring back home. He wanted to record his songs with his mates and so he put his money in that, which of course upset my mum because she wanted him to take some responsibility and look after us. She was still supporting the whole family. As I have already mentioned, I was in a new school and I wasn't in dance school so I had lost my happy place, too. In our first year of moving to that flat it was such a dark time on so many levels and I missed everything about my old life.

I think the other thing is, as a Russian, whenever there is

trouble, alcohol is never far away either. They both would drink. For my mum, however, it became a problem. It might have been an inherited thing from my grandfather perhaps, the alcohol, but in the end there was no hiding from the truth: Mum had turned into an alcoholic.

On the one hand, she was a very controlled, intelligent, good-looking woman and on the other, she was falling apart. Life at home was a misery, there was no money, she had a man who didn't care to be a father or a husband and I suppose drink was the only way she saw that she could let herself go. Maybe she thought it was the only way she could cope. She would invite lots of friends over to celebrate moving to our new home as she didn't want to be alone, but then it would become a day or two of celebrations and the drinking would continue. I think she gave up on a little bit of herself at that time, too. She was thirty-four years old and she knew her marriage was coming to an end. If life wasn't bad enough at that time, the other factor that broke my mum's spirit completely was that my grandmother was diagnosed with ovarian cancer. By the time it was diagnosed it was terminal and she wasn't going to live very much longer.

Mum went back to visit my grandmother in hospital every single day after work. She would wake up early, make lots of amazing, healthy food, which she would take to work and then take on to my grandmother. She would then get home very late and only have a few hours' sleep before doing it all again. Every night she would cry and my father, to give him his due, actually tried his hardest at this point. He tried to be there for her and offer his support as best he could, which I suppose helped in some small way.

I knew my grandmother was very sick but I didn't know she had cancer. She didn't know she had cancer either – my mother tried to hide it from her because she thought that she would give up psychologically if she realised just how sick she really was. It was awful, as she eventually found out when another woman on her ward read her medical notes and told her the truth. Can you imagine how dreadful that was? I remember my mum said to me that I had to go and visit her because she wasn't very well and I made some excuse that I didn't want to go because it seemed like a bit of a chore. But she insisted I went and then for a very long time afterwards, I went back to the old flat to see my grandparents on a regular basis. I also saw my friend Vera and it was sad as I still felt like this was home to me; this was my happy place.

I was pleased to be back in my old area and happy to visit my grandmother, even though she looked so poorly. That was the last thing I remember about her. After one visit I had come home and the next day, I don't know why, but I rang my mum at work. I can't remember why I needed to speak to her but I called and the person who answered told me she wasn't there because her mother had died. And that is how I found out about my grandmother: it was horrible. I thought to myself maybe it wasn't true or someone had made some kind of mistake. You don't want to believe something terrible like that has happened and you don't want to accept it.

That evening when my mum came home she didn't talk to me and I didn't talk to her – that way I didn't have to face up to the truth. But when she went to work the next day she must have realised that someone had told me the news, as when she came home later that evening she told me that it was true, that my grandmother had died. It was an awful time for my mother; she had lost the last person who had loved her no matter what. My dad also took my grandmother's death extremely badly – I think he always knew deep down that she was the one who was trying to help out between him and my mum. However angry Mum had got with him, it was always my grandmother who would be there to feed him, calm him down and try and make him feel better about himself. He loved her very, very much and she helped both my parents so much while they were young students and struggling. For a while, her death brought them together as they were both so upset over her passing and things at home were a little better.

In fairness, my mum really wasn't at home that much either as she was working so hard to try and support her family. It was a difficult time and not just for us, everyone was struggling. Mum then decided to quit her job shipbuilding in 1992 as she hadn't been paid for months and months and we could no longer continue. She needed money to support what was left of her family so she became a cleaner and a maid for a hotel. My mum, who had such an incredible education and was so clever, was washing floors. She would do shift patterns and it was decent pay compared to other jobs, but she was devastated as she felt degraded. However, we had to survive and so she had to do it.

Eventually I found a dance school in the centre of my town, which was just under half an hour's travel by public transport, and I started to go there. I can't tell you the relief when I started to dance again. I felt alive! My dance teachers were a married couple, Igor and Olga, and they were very good with all the students. Already they had established themselves as good teachers as the children they taught did well in competitions around the area. And they were very caring people, too. Olga was a former gymnast who used to tell us the story of when she was chosen to represent her age group in a big competition. She had previously hurt her knee very badly, but she was determined not to let anyone down and so she just taped her knee so tightly and carried on competing. Not taking part wasn't an option and she and Igor instilled this mantra, this sort of 'programming' into us right away – you can't let others down. You are part of a team, you put yourself second and you have to carry on whatever.

When I joined the school there was a boy already there who they thought I could dance with – he was thirteen and they said we could start competing straight away. But I felt a little out of my depth because I hadn't danced for over a year and this was a very good school. I didn't want to let anyone down either. Of course I wanted to compete, it was in my blood, but life at home was so bad – what with all the arguments and my mum drinking and trying to hold down a job as a cleaner. I did find it stressful trying to hide everything that was happening at home. I remember my first competition with this new boy, Maxim, and I had to borrow a couple of costumes from another girl – my mother couldn't afford to buy anything to make me a costume of my own.

We danced so well in the competition. It was only a local competition between the other dance schools in the area so nothing serious, but I was in an older dance category and so it felt wonderful. We came second or third and I should have felt so happy about that, I should have been so pleased, but I was so sad I didn't have anyone to share my joy with, so what was the point of being pleased with myself? My mum didn't come to watch as she was often drowning her sorrows with her girlfriends and Dad was hardly around.

I think this is when I realised that home to me was my dance school because my actual home wasn't a nice place to be. If my mum was at home, she wasn't in a good place as she was drinking and that would really upset me. But I suppose if there was any good to come of not wanting to go home, it was that my dancing improved very quickly as I was spending so much time at dance school!

Thankfully at that time, even though things were changing a lot in the country, there was still a good amount of money going into dance schools. My parents would not have been able to send me there if they had had to pay for it. We were lucky to have a roof over our heads really. At that point I realised that my father just didn't care about me, or what happened to me, which was a hard truth to face. I think I had a conversation with him at one point, when I was thirteen years old, and he told me he couldn't be with my mum any more because she was drinking all the time, and I then became angry with Mum because she was drinking a lot and she was degrading herself in my eyes. Here was this intelligent and beautiful person completely falling apart. Her behaviour was unrecognisable and she would be rude to me but it was because she was drunk all the time. She would be just sober enough to go to work at the hotel but as soon as she got back, she would drink.

Alcohol cost next to nothing in the early 1990s as the country was still completely in chaos. In Soviet Union times it was quite strongly monitored, but due to all the corruption you could buy a bottle of vodka quite cheaply. It was a horrible time:

at thirteen years old I felt completely alone and I was dealing with a mother who was an alcoholic. I will never forgive my dad for that – he should have been responsible. Years later my mum told me she felt that the biggest problem was that he should have taken her to the doctor and got her some help – but he didn't. All he would do was yell and shout that she was an embarrassment to him and herself because she was a drunk. How was that going to help a sick person? It didn't do any good, of course, her being shouted at and my father not trying to get her any help. Dad never made an effort to take her to a doctor. Instead he left me, just a child, to deal with it. He was weak, he didn't want to deal with it, perhaps he just didn't feel strong enough to deal with it, and so he left us. I think I heard from him a couple of times after that, on my birthday or something, but that was about it.

*****

So my life was pretty dark and the country wasn't faring much better either. The gap between rich and poor was becoming increasingly defined as those who worked high up in the government had bought all these closed-down factories for next to nothing and sold them to the highest bidders. By then it was all about making money rather than trying to help build up the country again. It tore Russia apart and for the poor, like my mother, it was hard. For normal, honest people it was very difficult. Doctors, engineers, teachers… they were all struggling as the government who used to pay their wages now didn't, which meant they had to find new jobs like cleaning floors or washing clothes to survive.

Vladivostok became an open city in 1991 so, in a way, my mum working at a hotel was quite good as the tourists tipped well. At that time it was all about survival, not living life. But we never starved – there was always some kind of food like rice or vegetables. You could buy other foods but they would be so, so expensive – for everyone. My mum had the advantage of still being young, too; she still had the ability to change her career, to work, to adapt, and although it was demoralising for her, she didn't have much choice. Any other jobs that she could do with her shipbuilding qualifications as an engineer weren't an option – the companies were now owned by private firms giving the work to other people less qualified and not so skilled – whoever they wanted to give them to, in all honesty. It was about who you knew and not what you knew and my mum was just a hard worker from a simple family. She didn't have any connections.

You could bribe your way into a job; you could buy yourself a diploma… corruption was all around us. The older generation struggled the most because they grew up in the Soviet Union system and had sixty years of savings in the bank from their working lives, thinking that when they retired they would have a decent amount to live on. But that all went wrong and their savings were lost and the price of medical care rocketed. There was no free healthcare system any more, which I think was most terrifying for them.

If the country and my home life were rubbish, at least I could say that dancing had once again been a blessing in my life. By now I had started teaching with Igor, who had asked me to help out in some of his lessons. I would assist him with his classes when he taught the five-year-olds and it was amazing as I was just fourteen years old and managing to earn a little bit of money. There was also a local theatre that was being used by a singer every evening and on some occasions she would want a theatrical feel to her show. So she came to the dance school to ask me and my partner to perform some background ballroom dances while she sang. She must have seen us in a competition or something somewhere and was happy to pay us a little, too. So I was earning from two different places, and at fourteen years old this was brilliant! For the first time I felt independent, and that I could spend a bit of money on myself as I had earned it.

And earning was something my mum wasn't doing as she eventually lost her job because she was drinking so much. She tried to get a few other jobs and because her education and credentials were so good, she could apply for better jobs in the hotel industry and lots of opportunities were open to her. But she couldn't keep any job as she slipped back to drink so easily. I think she had a weakness and as I have said before she might have inherited this addictive gene from my grandfather. She did try and get help quite a few times and tried several stints in rehab, but she would always have a relapse after a couple of months. The times she was in rehab I would be on my own at the flat and I can honestly say, even though I was only fourteen years old, I preferred living alone at that time than with her. Her drinking just caused arguments and then I would yell at her and she would be yelling at me – I was better on my own.

And I was good at hiding what was going on at home, too. I couldn't talk to anyone at school about it because I was too embarrassed and ashamed. And I think people at dance school knew by then that my parents had split up but I couldn't bring myself to talk to them about my mother being an alcoholic. For me it was too embarrassing to admit to anyone. If ever I was a bit low I think they just assumed it was because I was struggling without my dad being around.

As well as teaching, every moment I had was spent dancing; my partner and I would try and compete as much as possible. And there were times when my mum, who had just come out of rehab and was sober, would come and watch me and make an effort but then she would slip back to alcohol. Our relationship was so strained at that point: I hated her, and I hated being at home when she was there. This went on for the next two or three years so I would just try and be away from home as much as I could. So I did all the competitions that were available, especially if they were in different parts of the city. I loved being away from home. Not that it was a home with my mother; I think the last time I felt I had a home was when I was living with my grandparents. My survival mode became dancing and working and I felt as long as I had those things, I would be OK. Even now, if people ask me why I have done certain things or why I have made the decisions that I have, like sacrificing a relationship for a job, it stems back to this time in my childhood. I know people say I put my work above everything else but I think this is why: it was about survival. It made me feel normal, and dancing and teaching were ways of controlling my life and gave me something to focus on. I felt very isolated, too, because I was an only child and I didn't know how to deal with an alcoholic mother. So I focused instead on what made me happy, and that was dancing.

And you know what? When you're dancing, you can't think about anything else. You can't think about anything other than what you are doing, the steps you are making right at that moment, so it was a way I could escape into a different world.

And teaching those young children gave me such a real boost. I loved it and I was surrounded by their love, too. They were so open and wanted my praise so much. It made me feel useful and worthy and even though I felt I had no love at home, I was OK because I had children who wanted me to teach them. I had people who respected me as a dancer too, so I figured as long as I had that, I was OK. Emotionally I felt worthy and so I survived because I was making money and I was very careful with the little I earned.

I was paid in roubles so I couldn't say what that is now but with the teaching and being hired to dance in the shows, it was a good deal of money. In fact I could make as much in one night as my mum would make in a month when she was a maid. I think that is why I work so hard now, because I always have the fear of not being able to eat and being poor at the back of my mind. Also, I am able to provide for my mother now, which was something she couldn't do for me when I was younger.

She was a middle-aged woman who had lost her husband, lost her job and lost her mother all around the same time, so she turned to alcohol for help. Later she told me that she felt like she was drowning but she always thought I would be OK as I had dancing in my life. But for her, things were not OK at all, and one day she decided to try to commit suicide.

CHAPTER 7

The dark days

The day my mother tried to kill herself was the day when I knew I couldn't deal with this on my own any more: I had to tell someone. So I called my aunt, my grandad and my grandmother's sister, who was a doctor.

'I don't want to end up with a dead mother at home, you've got to help me,' I said.

So they did. It was a relief to tell them the true extent of her drinking and that I couldn't deal with it any more, that they needed to help me. I was just sixteen years old at the time. My aunt and grandad took her to rehab and she was there for about four months. They knew she was a drinker and they had been on her case in the past about it but they had no idea how bad it had got, absolutely no idea. My aunt would sometimes take my mum out for the evening and they would all end up drinking so I suppose she was aware of her reliance on alcohol but this was more than just reliance, this was a need to survive.

I will always remember that day she tried to commit suicide. I had come back after a couple of days away at a dance competition and she started arguing with me as soon as I came through the front door. She was completely drunk and I just didn't have the fight in me any more – I didn't need this the moment I got home. She was screaming at me and I was screaming at her and so I told her I hated her and didn't want to be around her any more. The next thing I knew she took a whole bunch of tablets – I think they were sleeping tablets, I couldn't tell you for certain. She just found them in the drawer and started taking them. I called the ambulance and then made her throw up all that she could and drink lots of water. The ambulance took her and put her on a drip and when she came back home from hospital, I made sure everyone was at the flat so we could confront her together.

She kept trying to tell us all that she didn't have a problem and that we just didn't understand what she was going through, and how hard it was for her that she had lost her mother. But as I had gathered everyone to be there at the flat when she got home, we started telling her some home truths – that she would lose me and she would lose them unless she tried to deal with her problems.

Enough was enough, and in the end my aunt and my grandfather took her to rehab in the suburbs of Vladivostok, to a place where the most severe addicts went.

I couldn't find it in my heart to visit her. I just didn't want to, so I woke up on my seventeenth birthday all by myself in the flat. That evening I invited some friends round from dance school and I cooked for everyone. They asked me where my mum was and I just said she was away – I didn't want anyone to know she was in rehab.

The truth was, while I was living on my own, I realised I was OK. Does that sound awful? I was OK with the thought that my relationship with my mother was broken for ever. In my mind, I thought we hated each other as we would always scream and shout at each other. And I blamed her for so much, too – for my terrible childhood, for my dad leaving, for being so aggressive and abusive towards me. It was a time in my life when I felt like, 'I can survive on my own. This is my life. I will dance and I will compete and I will survive.'

I honestly thought I would be on my own for ever but then I got a phone call from a doctor at the rehab clinic. He explained that he was a psychiatrist who was working with my mum and they had made lots of progress. Apparently she seemed to be in a very good place at the moment but they wanted me to come in and visit her.

But I couldn't do it. I was very honest with him and told him I didn't think I was up to it – how could I go there and visit her? I was doing OK by myself; I didn't want to go. And then he told me about what he had been working on with my mum over the past three months, and that the only reason she had given for wanting to live was me.

'There is no other reason apart from you that is keeping her going,' he explained. 'She has said over and over again that if she doesn't have a relationship with her daughter, she has no other reason to live.'

So I went. It was tough, *really* tough, as I felt like I was seeing a stranger. Mum didn't look like herself at all, she was so thin

– just a shell of herself really. She said she loved me and told me the only way she could continue with her life was with me. I can't really describe how I felt at that point – I still had a lot of anger towards her and deep down I didn't believe that she would change or that she would stop drinking. The psychiatrist explained that she had inherited a weakness for alcohol from her father and, although she had proven herself to be a very strong person during her time at the clinic, she needed to stick to the programme he had set out.

That was it. She came home a couple of weeks later, having been in rehab for about four months. It was hard to have her back in the flat – I was living with my mum but it was as if we were strangers. We were like two different women living together because I was an adult now, doing my own things. I had started at college and I had become quite independent, too.

I never really wanted to go to college because I thought it was a complete waste of time. I'd been earning money since I was fourteen years old so I couldn't see the point. And I was becoming popular with the kids I taught and their parents because they knew I was good and I cared about teaching them. In my heart I always knew dancing would be my profession and that I could make a living while teaching. But after finishing school, college was the next step. At least that was according to my mother. I had finished school with reasonable grades, mostly As in Literature, Russian Language, Biology and History, but I didn't fare quite so well in other subjects like Maths and Physics.

School had become a lot more relaxed since the break-up of

the Soviet Union. We no longer had to wear school uniform and the divide between rich and poor was never more evident. The children who came from rich families were wearing all these amazing, beautiful clothes and some of the teachers, who were struggling to feed their families with the poor wages they were getting, looked scruffy by comparison.

Whenever there was a school concert that would involve our school competing with others in the area, I was always the one chosen to represent the school in dancing competitions. The teachers encouraged it and they didn't mind quite so much if my grades slipped in certain subjects as I always did well for the school when it came to dancing! I didn't really have many friends either – as I have already mentioned, I found it hard to fit in when I moved schools and my main friendship group was always the people I met at dance school. I think the other kids thought I was a snob for not wanting to socialise with them but I just wasn't interested in boys or going to parties, I wanted to go and dance. At fourteen years old, when lots of girls began going out with boys and started smoking, drinking and having house parties, I was making money teaching. I did have one good friend called Lena, who was very musical and would be as passionate about music as I was about dancing. We both had strong hobbies that we loved and we couldn't see the point in boys or parties or anything like that so, in a way, I think that made us the subject of a lot of gossip – we were the two girls who weren't bothered about fitting in as we had our own lives outside of school. And I still had Vera as a friend. I was happy to have her friendship and guidance at school, too.

A few times in the last couple of years in school I found

love notes left on my locker, which was quite sweet. I used to try and figure out where they came from, but I didn't want a boyfriend: I was committed to dancing, not boys.

When I look back at those years, of Perestroika, of the Soviet Union's collapse, it is little wonder my generation is sometimes called 'The Lost Generation'. Kids of twelve or thirteen years old don't understand what is happening and they want to belong to something. At that age you have such a need to fit in and I had that same sense of wanting to belong, but I found it through dancing. Other friends at my school didn't have a path to follow and they would fall into gangs that would groom them for a life of crime. It was easy to see how they became lost, turned to drugs and fell into a world of desperation to somehow fit in. Seeing my friends like that affected me greatly. It is one of the main reasons I am so passionate about the charity work I do now with Dot Com Children's Foundation. Living through those times made me realise how vitally important the values of the foundation are in helping young people find a path in life. Children are desperate to have a sense of belonging which is why, although I couldn't help my friends, I am even more focused on helping children in society today with the values of dotcomcf.org. But I will explain more about that incredible charity later.

Back to schooling and me: my mum was adamant that I went to college. Education was everything to her so she was always on my case. It wasn't too bad because it was evening college and the lessons didn't interfere with dancing or teaching, but I just didn't see the point. I chose International Tourism Management as a degree as it was made up of all the subjects I loved – English, History, Geography, Russian Language, Sociology and Psychology.

Of course I don't regret it now. I am happy to say I am a college graduate. As dancers, we can quite often overlook things like that because we are so passionate about what we do. I don't know a lot of dancers with degrees because you just live your life as a dancer but it has helped me with what I do now to a certain extent, when I am working with different people on *Strictly Come Dancing*. You must find a way to click with the different personalities that you have to teach and the lessons I learnt in psychology during my college years certainly helped me. So would I have gone to college if it was a day course? No, I would have stood my ground with my mum! My argument would have been: 'Why should I give up my job for an education? You have an education and where has it got you?'

But I am grateful to her that she was persistent and in a way it made me want to complete college all the more because I could not bear to hear her moan about it: I did it for her. The moment I got that diploma I gave it straight to her and I said to her, 'Look, I have the degree! Now you can get off my case.'

CHAPTER 8

I grew up with an idea that any man in my life will always let me down...

Our country was a bleak place to be in the nineties. There was an endless circle of gang crime and violence and people getting shot on a daily basis. That sounds very dramatic, doesn't it? But it was the truth. It wasn't just bleak, it was downright scary and no one was above corruption, not even those who were meant to protect us. You could bribe the police – you could bribe anyone if you had the money. And you could buy and steal whatever you wanted if you were in a gang; no one touched you.

There is a story I want to tell you about a girlfriend of mine that shows what was happening at that time in my country. Her name was Oksanna and she was a gorgeous girl, inside and out. We became friends through another friend of mine and would often hang out at discos and other places. While studying at college, I was offered a position at a dance school in a city called Nakhodka, which was another small seaport near Vladivostok. It was one of the biggest dance schools in the area and the woman who was running it asked if I would 'try-out' with her son Eugene, who was my age and a very good dancer. She wanted us to compete together and thought I would be the perfect partner for him. Quite often that is how couples come together – the teachers or judges or owners of the dance schools are the ones who pair them up. They work out who will match whom and work best together.

It was a brilliant opportunity for me so I took it – although I had to promise my mum that I was only deferring my college course for one year and that I would definitely complete it as soon as I returned to Vladivostok. So I moved to Nakhodka to dance with Eugene, and Oksanna used to come and visit me and her grandmother, who also lived there. I was missing all my friends from Vladivostok so it was always nice to see her and we had some fun nights out together.

Nakhodka was about three hours' drive away and I think I went home most weekends when I wasn't competing to see Oksanna and my other friends. But about two weeks after one of her weekend visits to me, I got a call from my friend Irina. Absolutely distraught, she didn't know how to break the news to me that Oksanna had been killed. She had gone to a casino with her boyfriend, who was head of a fairly big, well-known gang, and they had both been shot as they left at 5am. Apparently she was just sitting in the car with him and someone shot them. They died from multiple gunshot wounds. Oksanna wasn't a target, she was in the wrong place at the wrong time, but nobody cared, they killed her anyway. The official story was that it was just a fight between two gangs but the police simply closed their eyes to it. No one wanted to deal with it or investigate it further, so her family never really got the justice they were owed. We had to bury a twenty-three-year-old friend and all of us, all of her girlfriends, helped her parents pay for the funeral.

I think it was after that when I realised I didn't want to live my life in Russia any more. It was a bit of a turning point for me, that tragedy, and I cried for a long time over Oksanna's death. Would I grow up in this country and suffer the same fate? Most of my other girlfriends, who were just twenty-one or twenty-two years old, were now married with babies. It might seem young now but then it was normal, everyone got married and some at just eighteen or nineteen years old, because that was the dream. It was a young girl's aspiration to be married to someone who had lots of money and power, even though it might come at a price. I'm not lying when I say I think around ninety per cent of my friends ended up being widows in those first two years of marriage, and were left alone with children and no money. I looked around and most of my girlfriends were widows at twenty years old, with young children and unable to pay for anything.

But it wasn't just that Vladivostok was rife with gang crime. Across Russia life was the same and I didn't want it to be *my* life. To be honest, getting married and having babies didn't appeal to me and as I had proved that I could earn money and support myself, I didn't want to give that up for a man. And what sort of man would it be, anyway? Probably a man who didn't think about what he was doing with his life, who just wanted to be part of a gang and didn't care about the danger it brought to his family. I suppose everyone tried to live their lives and make money any way they could, but I was used to standing on my own two feet – I never needed to depend on a man. And I loved dancing so much I knew it was going to be my career and in a way, my saviour. So I looked at my girlfriends, who had nothing going for them and no way to support themselves because their husbands or boyfriends had been killed, and it made me think about my own life. Grateful for what I had, it also reaffirmed to me that dancing was my way of life and I had to see where it was going to take me.

Being in Nakhodka and competing with Eugene also meant that I had to take a break from teaching and helping Igor and Olga. They had become like parents to me and although they were sad about me leaving, they recognised that it was an amazing opportunity for me to compete. It was because of going to Nakhodka that I was able to visit Japan and England through the competitions I entered at the school. I have a picture of me with The Beatles in Madame Tussauds and another one on a double-decker bus! I never thought I would end up living in England – it is so funny to look back at that time now and think how much my life has moved on.

Sadly, there was another tragedy around the corner for me. I had been in Nakhodka for nearly a year when I heard that Olga had been involved in a car crash with three of her girlfriends. She died a few days later in hospital. Once again I was devastated. She was my mentor in so many ways and I loved her. When she died she was only thirty-four years old and yet she was such a strong character. She was the one who kept the school running. Igor was a lovely man but it was Olga who was the driving force. She was the one making costumes for the dancers, teaching us hair and make-up, and the one we went to if ever we needed advice. She was a lovely, lovely woman and I had lost a person so dear to me. All the women I had grown up with or knew in Russia were very strong. They are their own breed, I suppose: Olga, my mum, who was strong enough to come out of her addiction, and then my grandmother, who dealt with an abusive husband. They very much shaped my understanding of men and I grew up with an idea that any man in your life will always let you down; you can't rely on them. That was my understanding of life in my early twenties: if you don't do it yourself or try to make a living yourself, you can't rely on anyone else.

I suppose that is why it was never my goal to be married and settled. Perhaps I never believed that it would happen or that any man would make me happy. I think I always thought that a man was weaker than a woman – even as a little girl I believed that. So how did it affect my future relationships? Well, it has made me very independent, which is something that most men don't like. It's funny, when you start a relationship, they like it, they like having an independent, confident woman. But they come to resent it a lot, too. In some ways I feel like I have always struggled to relax and breathe in a relationship – I can't seem to let myself be happy or settled. I always have a need to know where the next job is going to be and how I will earn my next pay cheque. It's a survival instinct in me and I guess that makes me quite a workaholic. And of course it has destroyed a lot of my relationships as I put work first. But you must understand that this was almost embedded in me from a little girl.

I dated some guys who might have changed my mind, whom I might have been able to let take care of me, but I never gave them a chance. A chance to show me that I could relax, that I could be looked after. I don't blame anyone for this ideology that I have, it is just the way I was raised. And back then I was addicted to my dancing and to teaching and competing. It made me feel worthy and above all else, happy. As a child I felt very unworthy because my parents didn't exactly make me feel like I was the centre of their world, so I was always craving some sort of admiration and I got that when I danced.

After Olga died, I went back to Vladivostok but I wasn't sad to be going home. My relationship with Eugene wasn't very healthy. He was, for want of a better word, a bully. He would push me around or slap me – that was just the way he was. He was an abusive man and to begin with I think that I put up with his behaviour because he was so great at dancing, and I thought this was something that I would just have to tolerate. Like many men in Russia he didn't have a very healthy relationship with alcohol and he would get drunk and then start saying something horrible. His mother knew about the abuse and I don't think I was the first partner that he had bullied. I told her that I wasn't going to carry on dancing with him if he continued to treat me the way he did and she was very upset. She told me I would be breaking up a very good partnership and that we had so much potential, but she could tell I wasn't bluffing; I would pack my bags and leave. And after one particularly nasty fight when he slapped me across the face I did just that.

It was the right time to return home to Vladivostok as Olga's death had affected Igor badly and he needed me to help and support him. Perhaps it wasn't surprising that he turned to drinking quite heavily as a way of dealing with his loss. But I couldn't turn my back on him – I felt responsible for him because he had always been so encouraging about my dancing and he and Olga had helped me so much. So it was at that point that I decided to step in and take over the running of the whole dance school. At twenty-two years old I started managing it and teaching full-time. I taught all the children and took them around the country just as I myself had been taken around. During the day I worked hard to keep the school up and running but I also went back to college to finish my diploma in the evenings. I didn't want to let Igor or the memory of Olga down as I felt so much loyalty to them, so it was then that I made the decision to stop competing, too. I decided I had to leave that part of me in Nakhodka and concentrate on the legacy that Olga had left. Around fifty children were attending the school in all sorts of dance categories and as well as teaching, I started judging in some of the smaller competitions, too.

Does this sound like a lot of responsibility? I think nowadays it probably sounds crazy, a twenty-something with no qualifications and fresh out of school herself in charge of a dance school. But I was so grateful to Olga and Igor for everything they had done for me that it was a very natural course of action. Igor gave me my first teaching experience when I was just fourteen – that was a massive opportunity and one I will always be thankful for. He and Olga were always there for me; I'm sure they must have figured out my home life wasn't much fun and so they took me under their wing. It wouldn't have taken much figuring out – when all the other dancers had their parents come and watch them in competitions and cheer them on, I had no one in the audience. So they made an extra effort to support me and they focused my passion for dancing. There was a huge level of trust as well, as they could see that I really loved teaching the younger ones even though I wasn't much more than a child myself. So they encouraged it.

Of course my love for competing never went away. No matter how much responsibility I had for the school, I suppose I knew that I wasn't done with competing just yet. It is a belief of mine that sometimes you have to be brave enough to take an opportunity when it comes up and it wasn't long before I had the chance to make a life-altering decision.

CHAPTER 9

A boy called Brian...

Despite his bullying ways, I did get the chance to take part in a lot of competitions with Eugene while dancing in Nakhodka. Eugene's mum took us to compete in Japan and we always visited one particular school when we were there for our shows. I remember one teacher, Mr Kobaici, who would watch us and was always very encouraging. After leaving Nakhodka and having made the decision to put my competing days behind me, I didn't think much more about him, so it was nice to bump into him when he travelled to Vladivostok to the big dance competition that is always held there every year in July. I was there with some of the students from my school and I knew he always brought some of his better pupils from Japan to compete, as Vladivostok was by then an open city so there was the opportunity for lots of different nationalities to enter.

Mr Kobaici spoke a bit of broken Russian as he was always

working with Russian dancers but he had travelled over with a translator too, and when he saw me, he came over right away. With his translator's help, he told me he thought it was a shame I wasn't competing any more and that I had let the teaching take over.

'Remember Julia?' he said.

Julia was a girl whom I known since I was little and had danced with from a young age. She was originally from St Petersburg and her mum was a dance teacher as well. I knew that her mum and Eugene's mum were friends and Julia was invited to come to the dance school in Nakhodka too, where she competed and was very good. But she didn't like being away from home and went back to be with her parents in St Petersburg. As far as I was aware, that was what she had last been doing, but I was wrong.

'Julia is an American champion,' he told me. 'She moved to America and married her dance partner and now they are the champions in a Latin category called American Rhythm.'

I was absolutely stunned. Until then I had no idea how well she had done for herself and I was thrilled for her. She and her partner, Bob Powers, were very successful and Mr Kobaici told me he was going to America shortly to watch her perform in one of the big competitions held in Miami called the Nationals.

'Do you want to write to her?' he asked me. 'I will make sure she gets it if you do.'

So I wrote her a letter, which basically said:

Hi Julia, do you remember me? This is mad! I am so very happy for you as you always wanted to compete and be successful. If there is anything ever that comes up that you

*think I could do as a job let me know as I know you travel a
lot and compete and know a lot of people. Thanks, Kristina*

I had nothing to lose in writing that letter and I didn't think for
one second I would get an answer. That was in July 2000 and
I knew that the Nationals were always held in the first week in
September. At the end of September I got a letter from Julia:

*Hi Kristina! Yes, I live in Arizona with my husband, Bob,
now. We met in St Petersburg as he had come over to do
a show with some other American dancers and we had
a try-out and things just went from there. I then moved
to the States and I have been here for the past six years.
In answer to your question, I don't know anyone who is
looking for a partner but if I do, I will let you know.
Would you be interested in teaching? There are a lot of
Russians over here now since the Soviet Union broke up
and there are lots of Russian dance schools looking for
teachers. Do let me know. Julia*

I wrote back and said of course I would be interested and
it would be great if she could keep me in mind; I put the
telephone number of my flat at the bottom. Then in October I
got a phone call from her, although it took me a while to work
out who it was – she now had a thick American accent. She
told me about a dance studio in New York that was looking
for teachers and asked if I would be interested in going. There
were lots of Russian kids in New York who needed a Russian
teacher but there would be no opportunity to compete or dance
myself, it would just be a teaching position. She would put me

in touch with the owners of the school who were very nice and encouraging and had said they would arrange a visa for me if I was going to accept the position.

I told her I wanted to think about it and although I was interested, at the same time it was so scary, the thought of moving to America and leaving my mum and all my friends behind. And I couldn't speak more than a few words of English. Maybe someone else would have jumped at the chance, but I was already teaching and besides, I had so much loyalty to my dance school and Igor. I didn't want to give them up for just another teaching position. Yes, I suppose this was a once-in-a-lifetime opportunity but my dream wasn't just to move to America. My dream was dancing and it didn't matter which country it took me to.

So I said no. I told the New York dance school that I would like to compete as well as teach and I didn't want to leave the school I was teaching at. And, if I'm being honest, I didn't want to leave my mum either. She was very encouraging and I know if I had decided to move then she would have supported me. But I think she was glad that I decided not to go – she had been fussing about the fact that I wouldn't know anyone, I didn't speak English and I would be on my own.

I did write to Julia to explain why I had turned the job down and, to be honest, I then put any thoughts of going to America to compete out of my mind. So it was a complete surprise to get a phone call from her in November with some exciting news. She explained that she had been teaching a boy from Seattle who had an older partner who didn't want to carry on competing any more. His name was Brian, he was twenty-four years old and he was 'the loveliest boy ever,' she said. She also

Top left: My maternal grandmother, Valentina Vorobieva.

Top right: Grigory, my grandfather and Valentina's first husband.

Middle left: My parents on their wedding day in 1977.

Middle right: Mum looking beautiful in 1983.

Right: Smile for the camera! Dad, Mum (who is pregnant with me), Grandmother Valentina, Grandfather Boris and my aunt Valeria.

Above left: In happy times: my mother and I in 1978.

Above right: Playing at kindergarten with my grandmother Marina, who looked after me in Holmsk.

Below: With my parents in 1980.

Above left: A children's party to celebrate New Year in 1982. I am crouched in the centre, dressed as a snow queen.

Above right: On holiday in 1983.

Below left: New Year celebrations with my parents in 1986.

Below right: On a summer camp holiday in Shmakovka later that year.

Above left: All smiles on my first day at school.

Above right: In my school uniform standing next to a picture of Lenin. His portrait hung in every classroom.

Below: My class with our very strict teacher. I am second from the right on the front row – how happy I look!

Above left: With my first dance partner Roman at our first competition. My mum spent all night making my dress.

Above right: I have always loved performing. Here I am in traditional dress dancing to an accordion.

Below left and right: At another competition in a dress my mum sewed for me.

Above: With my dance teachers in Vladivostok, husband and wife Igor and Olga.

Below left: Winning first place in a competition in Japan with my dance partner from Nakhodka, Eugene. I am in the blue dress.

Below right: It was when competing with Eugene in Japan that I first met Mr Kobaici.

Above left: My first visit to London aged twenty. I never dreamed I'd be one day living there!

Above right: With some of my students in Russia, not long before I moved to Seattle.

Below: I loved teaching and the students were wonderful but Igor was very supportive of my decision to move to the USA.

Above: With my dance partner Brian at our first competition in the USA in 2002. We are pictured here with his family – my American family – brother Sean, dad Ron and mum Kathy.

Below left: Placing third at the United States Dance Championships in 2003.

Below right: The couple in black: competing with Brian in 2003.

said he was very committed to dancing but was adamant that he only wanted to dance with a Russian girl as he thought that was the only way he would be able to win any competitions! It wasn't surprising though, she added, as he had always been taught by her and her husband Bob and had seen how successful they were. In his mind, she said, he obviously thought this was the way to win – to get a Russian partner!

The other bit of news was that Brian's dance school in Seattle was also looking for a teacher so I would be able to do a little bit of teaching as well as competing. It sounded too good to be true, but there was no way I could move to America to dance with a boy I hadn't even met, let alone danced with.

So I asked Julia: 'What if Brian doesn't like me? What if I don't like him? What if we don't click as a dance couple?' It all seemed too much of a big risk.

So Julia suggested we do what is called a 'try-out', which is a very common thing in this business. Normally, you would have a teacher recommend a pairing and you would put a few routines together to see if you had the potential to work as the perfect dance couple.

'Of course I would love to meet him for a try-out,' I told Julia, 'but I don't have the finances to travel to America and I don't have a visa either – and probably wouldn't get one on the basis that I was just travelling to America to try and see if I was suitable to dance with an American boy.'

Julia understood and so she decided to talk to Brian to see what he wanted to do. But Brian was so completely adamant that he would only dance with a Russian girl that he told her he would happily travel to Russia to meet me. It was unbelievable really, but he was very focused on what he wanted. With help from his family, in January 2001 I found myself waiting at the airport to meet what might be my new dance partner.

*****

We were in the midst of an extremely harsh winter and January that year was bitterly cold. As I didn't speak any English, I invited one of my friends who studied English in college to come with me to the airport to be my translator. And I had my mum with us, too.

I remember spotting Brian and just thinking, 'Oh. My. God!' – for no reason other than that this poor boy had just wandered out of the airport in the thinnest Nike coat I have ever seen and was desperately trying not to look like he was frozen in our -20 degrees climate. We hurried him into the car and he was absolutely freezing. It took him a while to stop shivering and he said he couldn't believe the amount of ice and snow everywhere.

Once he felt warm enough to start talking, he told my friend that he hadn't quite realised where he was going in Russia when he agreed to a try-out after Julia asked him. He had assumed I was from St Petersburg, where Julia is from, in the more central part of Russia. Then he realised I was in Vladivostok and he said he had to look on the map and his dad pointed out that I lived at the very last stop of the Trans-Siberian Railway. They couldn't believe I was at the very end of Russia and assumed it was the end of the world, where bears would be walking down the street and tigers might appear at the side of the road! It was all quite funny really, and Brian was very sweet and so very eager. He wanted to get to the dance school as soon as possible so we dropped him off at the hotel so he could freshen up – and warm up! And then I think it was just two hours later when we went to my dance school. We did some rehearsing and the first thing that struck me was that we both had very different styles of dancing. The training you get in Russia is all about technique and precision while he was a very natural dancer and there was a lot less structure to his moves. I think we danced the cha-cha-cha. It was fun, he was very warm and sweet and very complimentary of my dance skills.

That evening I had group classes to teach and he asked if he could stay and watch, which I thought was funny as he couldn't understand a word of Russian! But he wanted to stay and my friend who was acting as the translator was happy to stay and watch, too. Afterwards, we all went back to see my mum at the flat and have something to eat. Mum was cooking like crazy and wanted to feed him all this delicious Russian food so he could experience her homemade dishes. He stayed for about three days in Vladivostok and we spent more time dancing as well as doing a bit of sightseeing. Later he told me that all he remembers about coming over to meet me at that time was how cold it was and that he'd never seen a frozen sea before – so the dancing obviously made a big impact! The funny thing was, he lived in Seattle, which is a seaport as well and it rains a lot of the time, but apparently the weather he experienced in Russia made a lasting impression.

After being with me for three days he told me that he would like to organise my visa to come to America and that he really wanted us to compete together. So he went back to Seattle to talk to the dance studio owners and talk to his parents – they would have to become my sponsors in order for me to be granted a visa. I would have to live with him and his family and I had to know they were all happy about that. To be honest, I didn't think I would get the visa and all my friends kept telling me not to get my hopes up as lots of people we knew had tried to move to the States but had been refused. I was led to believe it was still a fairly difficult process. But my passion for competing had been reignited and I knew that life was too short not to give it a try, even if I was refused. I was only twenty-three years old, this was my time to compete and I could always fall back on teaching at any age. Igor was very supportive, however hard he might have found the prospect of me going, and he said to me, 'Kristina, what are you doing here? Why are you still here teaching? Go and compete!'

I was pleased. He was obviously very sad to be letting me go as I had been such a big help to him, but he understood that this was a great opportunity. But there was still a big part of me that couldn't quite get my head around leaving Russia. I spoke no English and I had no money so how would I get on in America? Brian and I began exchanging letters, and if he called me I made sure my friend was there to translate. He would explain to her how it would all work logistically, which at least helped me understand the reality of moving to the States.

I had to go to Moscow to apply for my visa – although we have an American Embassy in Vladivostok they didn't deal with visas – so it felt like a long process. Once there I had several meetings and they took my fingerprints and I had to chat to a lot of people. You are then given a date to return to the Embassy to collect your passport, which has with it either a granted visa or a refusal letter. Now I can't begin to tell you how happy I was when I returned and I saw this visa with all my paperwork! I was so over the moon and I really felt that somehow I had had help from the hand of Fate or from God, or something. When you do believe and when you want to do something so much, sometimes it can all just come together. Moving to America wasn't my goal or my dream but to continue doing what I loved – dancing and competing – was, and it was coming true.

Of course Mum was happy for me but she was very sad at the same time. She knew that in my heart this is what I wanted, though.

'You can't sit here at twenty-three years old, teaching children and thinking "What if?"' she told me. 'You've got to try so you have to go. You have a nice family to live with and you will have Julia too, who will always support you.'

Did I worry that my mum would go back to drinking once I had gone? To be honest, I had nightmares for a long, long time where I would see an image of her, standing in our kitchen, drinking. That was where she always was, drinking in the kitchen. So yes, it frightened me that she would go back to those ways. But she wasn't in a bad place at that time – she had a nice man who was very supportive in her life. And he did what my dad didn't do: he took very good care of her. He drove her to her AA meetings and her therapy sessions and she completed all the steps and eventually decided that was that, she didn't need it any more. She did it the right way and he was wonderful and I know he was a great support to her. He genuinely cared for her and even though they are not in a relationship any more, they are still good friends.

Mum had officially divorced on 11 March 1999, two years before I moved to America. I don't think there was any great rush to get it done before, it was just paperwork, although my dad remarried the same year so I think he had to show his official divorce papers before he could apply to get married again. It was just a formality really – my mum kept the flat and my dad got the divorce he needed. Many times over the years I asked Mum why she never remarried, but she always told me that she didn't want me to be raised by another man. She said she was fighting for me to have my own father take responsibility, she wanted him to realise he was a dad and that he was the one who had to act like one. It is only now that she has admitted that she should have found someone else. Apparently for many, many years she didn't think she would want another child as she thought one was plenty! But she has since told me that not having another child and starting a family with another man is her only regret. It wasn't as if she was short of admirers, either. There were a couple of men around who were very much in love with her and wanted to adopt me, marry her and make a proper family, but she never accepted them.

My dad had no idea that I was leaving Russia. By then I had no contact with him at all. I remember Mum telling me that she had heard he had remarried but he was never interested in finding out what was happening in my life so I wasn't that fussed about his. I received no letters, no contact, nothing: absolutely nothing. And he didn't know I had left for America until a mutual friend told him and suddenly my mum got a phone call and he wanted to know what was going on and why wasn't he told about me leaving the country? She told him it was because he never tried to contact me. He never made any effort to be in my life or to support me or be a father figure in any kind of way, so why would I tell him?

He did ask for my address in America, which my mum gave

him, and he wrote me a letter. I still have it somewhere, I think. In it he asked for forgiveness – for me to forgive him for the things he had done wrong, for being a bad father, for not being there for me. I was his only daughter and he said he regretted not making any effort. I don't know what to say about it really. Yes, it was nice to receive the letter but I can't say it made me feel anything for him. I forgive him most things, I don't carry grudges in life, but I will never forget how he made me feel when I was just a child. I think the pain and the grief when he left me all those times, and then when he left at the most difficult time in my life, when my mum was so low and he saw me struggling to deal with her on my own, I will never forgive him for that. I should never have had to deal with that.

He was obviously saying to all his friends that he couldn't live with my mother because she was always drinking, but she was always drinking because they were so unhappy. He never made any effort to take her to the doctor and he never made her feel that he cared – not even caring in the most basic form, one human being for another. And they were husband and wife! Then there was my mum, who had made so much effort to make our relationship work again, that was what mattered to me now. So yes, it was nice to receive his letter but I didn't want to have him back in my life. Besides, my life was about to head off in a completely new direction. In May 2001, I was ready to start my new adventure in America…

CHAPTER 10

Smiling at strangers? I'm a long way from home...

I remember the day I left Russia for America. My mum was crying her eyes out at the airport and I knew saying goodbye to her was going to be tough, but I didn't realise quite how upsetting it would be. In my heart I knew I was making the right decision, this was my dream, but saying goodbye to my mum, my aunt and Grandad Boris, and my best friend Irina in a dreary airport surrounded by lots of people bustling by was very hard. I tried to reassure myself that not only would I be able to make a good living in America, I would be able to help my mum out financially, too. It was a big part of why I agreed to go, the potential to make money for my family was too good an opportunity to turn down. But even with that sensible idea in my head, it didn't make waving goodbye to Mum any easier. And not knowing when I might see her again was especially hard. But I boarded that flight and that was that, next stop

Seattle! It was time to find out if I had just made the best or worst decision of my life…

The moment the plane touched down in Seattle I knew I was going to be OK. Brian and his family – his mum, dad and brother Sean – were all waiting for me at the arrival gates with a big poster that said 'Welcome To America' and balloons and they were waving an American flag, too. It was very sweet, and right from day one they made me feel part of their incredibly warm, wonderful family. For me the one scary thing was that I could only say my name. I couldn't speak any English so even though they made me feel welcome inside, I couldn't thank them or talk to them and therefore settle into their world completely. Kathy, Brian's mum, was a school teacher so she spoke very slowly to try and communicate with me but it didn't really do much good at first, so we used signs and pointing to convey what we needed to. And I could not understand his dad at all – Ron had a very typical thick American accent and Brian and Sean were young and used a lot of slang, which meant I didn't understand them either for a long, long time. But they were so good to me; they took me around Seattle the first day I arrived and I remember it was a beautiful warm day. They had a wonderful house in West Seattle overlooking the sea and you could see the port and the cargo ships coming in.

I remember spotting a ship with a Vladivostok logo on it from one of our shipping companies and I felt like I was at home! It was a good feeling and I rang my mum to let her know I had arrived safely and that I could see the sea and how lovely Brian's family were. She told me she hadn't slept since I left and how lonely she was in the flat without me, which I didn't really want to hear as it just made me feel terribly sad. I told her I loved her and we would speak again soon and then I tried to focus on my new life.

The next day we went to the dance school and started our first round of rehearsals. That was it! There was no time like the present, I was there for a reason, and so we got on with training straight away. The first couple of weeks were very exciting – we were meeting new people but I was still a little overwhelmed by it all as I was sometimes struggling to work out what was going on, and I think I spent most of my time pointing and nodding a lot! But it didn't take me long to understand the basic stuff, like whether I wanted food or needed a drink, and then Julia got in contact with me and we arranged to have some lessons with her and Bob in Arizona in those first few weeks, too. That was exciting! I was really looking forward to seeing Julia and speaking Russian with someone.

It's funny how language can be such a barrier. However hard you try to communicate in different ways, not speaking to a person can make you feel very isolated. Sometimes it's not just day-to-day communications that are the problem, it is expressing thoughts or feelings. At times I just wanted to say that I wanted to be alone with my thoughts but how can you express that?

In those first couple of weeks I met a lot of Brian's friends and apparently they all asked him if I was upset about something. Brian said I was fine but they weren't convinced because they couldn't understand why I was not smiling! It was very strange and Brian did try and explain to me that in America, people just smile – at strangers on the streets even, or if you are in a shop. I found that very strange and I remember one day just walking down the road and I saw a couple of women walking their dogs and they were smiling at me. 'This is so weird,' I thought. 'In Russia you just don't do that, especially to random strangers. It would be very odd!' But Brian explained that this is what people do in America and you have to smile otherwise they think you are upset or being rude and you didn't want to be perceived as a rude person. Well, that was a big culture shock but I certainly didn't want to walk around with a big smile on my face the whole time, it felt very unnatural and weird! Brian kept telling me it was a polite thing to do, but I just couldn't do it. When I told my mum she didn't get it either.

In those first few months I wrote to my mum a lot and, looking back at my letters now, I can see just how sad and lonely I must have felt. I did admit to her that I was finding it very hard being away from home and I didn't know if I could stay there much longer. I don't like to admit defeat in anything but I felt so alone. Of course to begin with it was exciting, but the reality soon hit that I was a foreigner in a strange country and I had no friends or family either. I think Americans are under the impression that people long to move to the States and people have to be happy when they are here as they are moving to this wonderful country. Don't get me wrong, Brian's family were wonderful. I felt loved and accepted and I will always be grateful to them as they made me feel so welcome and part of their family.

But I was scared of going to the shop – if someone asked me something, I wouldn't know what to say. So in a way, I spent more time with Brian than just rehearsing and dancing as I relied on him a lot. Every morning he drove us to rehearsals, where we would learn our routines and then, as he was teaching in the afternoon, he would drive me home and afterwards go back to school for his class. I wanted to feel useful and as his mum and dad both worked and Sean was at college, I decided to use my time alone cooking and cleaning. And they loved my cooking – I just used whatever I could find in the fridge and it made me feel like I was pulling my weight, too.

Kathy was such a wonderful mum; she was always putting everyone else's needs ahead of hers. She would come home after long days at the school where she worked, a school for children with behavioural difficulties, and then cook the dinner or do the laundry and tidy up and then do paperwork. I don't know when she slept! So if there were any little things I could do to help, I would do. She once caught me doing all the dishes and tried to explain they had a dishwasher. Well, I had never seen a dishwasher before so I didn't have a clue! I didn't know what it was or how to use one so they had to teach me.

They also tried to help me learn English, too. I had brought a lot of books over from Russia to try and help with the language and I found reading a good way to learn. Every evening they insisted I watch a film with them and they would put the English subtitles on so I could read and watch. I was dreadful at writing and spelling in English but I could read it OK and it helped me learn to speak it, too. They also enrolled me in a specialist school where English was taught as a second language, but as it was an evening class and we were in training a lot, it didn't really work out. I had to rely on a lift to and from the classes so I only went for about a month in the end. Speaking gradually became a bit easier as I was constantly picking up words from listening to conversations. And then I started teaching, which helped. I began with only a couple of lessons a week but it gave me a bit of confidence, too. Brian and I also taught together as a couple. We would teach salsa as it was very popular in America and lots of the community colleges offered these classes. It was fun! I hadn't ever danced salsa before whereas Brian loved it, and he took me to salsa clubs to show me what it was like. It was like a *Dirty Dancing* experience! Honestly, I was like the Baby character, sitting in the corner watching all these people shaking their bits at each other. I was used to very rigid, very strict techniques, and this was just freestyle, which I hadn't done a lot of before. At first I was adamant I wasn't going to do that sort of dancing – it just wasn't me – but eventually the music got to me. It is so infectious, you can't sit still when it's on, and so I started to dance it. You could say I had 'The Time of My Life'!

With the help of Julia and Bob, Brian and I started putting routines together. It was a little challenging to begin with as our style of dancing was very different – he had a very freestyle, salsa rhythm and I came from a strong ballroom and Latin background, which was very structured. And I had been competing since I was six or seven years old, taking part in fairly big competitions all over the world, whereas Brian started dancing socially and fell in love with it, but taking part in competitions was a relatively new experience for him. He had actually only done a few competitions and those were in the past couple of years at a local level so our experiences of being judged were very different, too. I think I had assumed he had a similar background to me, and we certainly didn't discuss it when we met in Vladivostok as he was only with me for three days.

So seeing Bob and Julia would be a huge help as they would be able to put our routines together and merge both our styles effectively. There weren't many professional dancers in Seattle then. There were a lot of amateurs and a lot of kids wanting to learn, but it wasn't a massive scene for professional dancers. Most of them lived in the big cities like Los Angeles, New York and Boston and the only other competitive couple that we knew of in our area was two teachers.

It's funny, even though my grasp of the English language wasn't brilliant, there was no misunderstanding the icy vibe I received from the woman when we met. Maybe she was upset that there was another couple to compete with in what they saw as their territory, their dance studio, and she was jealous, but whatever the reason she wasn't very friendly at all. It did make me feel quite upset: already I felt vulnerable being in a different country and the last thing I wanted was to be made to feel unwelcome at the dance rooms. But she wasn't subtle in her dislike for me, she didn't talk to me and she looked down on Brian and me, too. Brian realised it as well but he wasn't at all bothered. 'Don't mind, don't care!' he would tell me. 'Just be the best we can be, forget them.'

I remember they asked me if Brian and I would be taking part in one of the competitions that was coming up in Seattle – I think they must have been worried we would be going up against them in the same category. It occurred to me that the woman could see potential in us as a couple and she was jealous that we might be a better pair. I wasn't at all surprised – there is a lot of jealousy in the world of ballroom dancing because it is so highly competitive. But I was always brought up with the idea that I just had to concentrate on being the best I could be. In Russia our teachers kept drumming into us the idea that you couldn't think about anything else other than who you are as a dancer. This is what people will judge you on, your skills on the dance floor, and if you do your best then your work will speak for itself. But it seemed the world of professional dancing wasn't just about being an amazing dancer: there was quite a lot of politics and bribery involved, too. Unfortunately, Brian and I learnt the hard way that our dedication to training and rehearsals wasn't going to win us any medals unless we 'played the game'.

CHAPTER 11

Happy holidays – the American way!

Brian and I didn't take part in the competition in Seattle as it was too early for us to be competing and we didn't want to rush, so instead we flew to Arizona to see Bob and Julia. It was lovely to see her and reminisce about growing up in Russia and our childhood. And it did make me realise how much I was missing home – my friends and family of course, but also my culture and simple things like the food. I felt quite nostalgic about lots of things, and I spoke Russian for the whole weekend we were with Julia, which was great. The lifestyle that Bob and Julia had was inspiring. They lived in a beautiful big house, had fast cars and a wonderfully big dance studio – all from being champions and very famous in their world.

'I could be like this, too,' I thought. 'I could be this successful and make my move to America worthwhile. I just have to keep training, to keep doing my best.'

Brian felt the same but he took it too far: he put the dream of being the next Bob and Julia on such a pedestal that it ended up putting too much pressure on us as Brian and Kristina. He wanted to be them so much it ended up overshadowing everything we did and what was an aspiring dream to begin with soon became an addiction.

But the weekend away in Arizona did motivate us both and Julia and Bob worked on our routines and encouraged us to start doing a few smaller competitions. It was the only way to practise our routines properly and work out what the judges liked or what we could change. We went back to Seattle full of enthusiasm and determined to do well. Brian was paying for everything at that time – I wasn't earning a lot teaching the few lessons I did and he was so caught up in the idea of us being champions that he put all of his money, all of his savings, into us as a dance couple. He wanted to give everything he had for the chance to be a champion and I have a lot to thank him for. He brought me to America and changed my life and at no point lost any enthusiasm or focus on his goal.

A wonderful boy, he was raised in a very good family, a family for whom the children were everything. Ron and Kathy lived their lives through Brian and Sean and they were both so giving in every single way. It must have been difficult for them and a lot of responsibility, too, having me live with them. They were driving me everywhere and paying for everything but they never, ever made me feel like I owed them anything. They always made me feel so loved and welcome and like a daughter really.

It was a beautiful time for me: all those years I had longed for a proper family with proper parents and here was one with so much love to give. For the first time since I had moved out of my grandparents' flat when I was twelve years old, I felt happy and settled. But boy, did I have a lot to learn about the American culture! Christmas is a good example. I just could not for the life of me understand why they started putting up the Christmas tree in the middle of December. In Russia, Christmas is a religious holiday, and in Orthodox Christianity, Christmas is 7 January. So our main holiday is really New Year's Eve and we call our tree a New Year tree. We put it up and put all our presents underneath it on New Year's Eve. And then after midnight we give each other our presents to celebrate new beginnings, new life, a new year.

An American Christmas is very different. When they brought the tree home and they kept calling it a Christmas tree, I kept calling it a New Year tree and they were laughing at me. So I tried to explain how it worked in Russia and they were trying to explain how it worked in America! But it was a lot of fun and every year I lived with them we celebrated both their Christmas and the Russian Christmas, which was very kind. And boy, was I spoilt rotten on my first Christmas! They completely showered me with presents. I woke up on Christmas Day to find these amazing parcels, all beautifully wrapped, and a day filled with such delicious food. I thought I would end up the size of a big turkey myself, the amount I ate!

Over the years my mum came for Christmas and it was always special to have her be part of the celebrations. It was very calming and it did feel like we were one big happy family. She would come over for a good two or three weeks and it was nice to have her around and we made sure we did plenty of traditional Russian cooking for the family, which they absolutely loved. Christmas was such a big occasion for them. Kathy had boxes of different ornaments that she would put up everywhere and the whole house would be covered! Everything was full-on.

I soon realised that Americans didn't do things by halves at Christmas. Brian would put together a nativity scene that would take up the whole table and he'd buy a new piece for it each year so it just grew and grew. And Ron would put up all these lights outside the house that seemed to light up the whole street. It wasn't just Brian's family, though – everyone seemed to get into the spirit of Christmas. We would drive around the neighbourhood and see all the houses with lights and it was magical. I never saw anything like that in Russia. It was completely different, and Mum loved it, too. I have so many happy memories of Christmastime with Brian's family, which is something that I don't really have from my childhood. I love Christmas, don't get me wrong, but I can't really remember many happy ones in Russia. For Brian and his family, it was spending time together and being happy that made it special. I will be forever thankful for those memories.

While being part of a family was just what I needed, it made me realise how much I could help my own family, too. As soon as I came to America I went to the bank, opened an account and had two cards made. I then Fed-Exed one over to my mum so she could go and take any money she needed from my account. Any money I earned, from a little bit of teaching, say, I could put into that account and she could use. It was all about supporting my mum for I knew what a tough life she had. As an athlete you are quite selfish by nature – you go where the competitions are, where you can concentrate on being the best, wherever that may be – and your family can be left behind. But they are your family and they don't ever complain. I moved to the States purely to follow my dancing dream, so yes, it was a selfish move because it was what I wanted to do.

I remember I had been in America about a year when I travelled back to Russia to visit my mum and my aunt. By then I was quite homesick so I needed to go back to my own world, if that makes sense. But I didn't realise until I landed just how comfortable I had become with life in America. It hit me straight away: how could I have forgotten how different and difficult life in Russia is? It is a different world to America. Everything is a struggle in Russia, people will do anything they can to make ends meet and support their families.

I went to visit my aunt, who was still living in the same flat in Vladivostok where I had lived with her when I was younger, and still with Grandad Boris, too. But she was a single mother now after her husband died of a stroke and she was bringing up her two young children completely alone. Even with government support as a single parent, she was barely getting enough money to feed her family and she couldn't really work as she was always looking after them. My mum would help by going to babysit so she might be able to do some part-time work but it was hard. There was no way I couldn't help her, they were my family as well, and I got cross with myself for living in another country for so little time and already forgetting how much of a struggle life is for my own family in my own country. So I started sending money to my aunt, too, who of course was more like a sister to me.

I couldn't cope with seeing them struggle and I feel blessed that the work I do, not only do I love, but it also allows me to earn good money and help my family. And I will continue to support them for as long as they need me; that is what family is all about. Anyway, there is no one else to help them! My aunt never remarried and she dedicated her life to her two children, sacrificing her own happiness. I suppose she didn't want to date anyone when her primary concern was always for her children. My grandad is still working; soon he will be eighty years old and he can't stop working as he feels he needs to keep earning money to help my aunt. We all feel a sense of duty to help our family and so we do: it's as simple as that.

So while that first year in Seattle was hard in some respects it was also a time when I felt very loved, very looked after and very privileged. I also met my best friend out there, Alex. She is still living in Seattle and I always try and visit her at least once a year. I am godmother to her son Maxim, too. I met her when she came to me for dance lessons, around nine months after I had moved to the States, and we have been friends ever since.

But making friends and being a family wasn't my mission when I left Russia, it was to dance and to compete and to do well. So Brian and I took part in a few competitions just to get started and we flew to Arizona to do a small one alongside Bob and Julia. I found a woman in Seattle who owned a big dance club and made dance costumes so I was able to have a couple of dresses made for the competitions, which was very exciting. Every year in September there is a big competition called the Nationals. It is held in Miami and Brian and I decided it was time for us to go and watch and show everyone that there was a new couple on the scene: we were the new dancers in town!

But the Nationals weren't held that year as on 11 September

2001 terrorists attacked New York City and they cancelled the competition as there were no planes flying anywhere in the country. For me 9/11 was a very strange situation for one reason alone: I could completely understand why a country felt so aggrieved over a terrorist attack on its own soil, but I couldn't fathom how they could watch other countries on the news being bombed or attacked and not seem to care. There were so many things happening in Russia – schools were being bombed in Moscow and there was a lot fighting in Chechnya. So when it happened in New York, I remember telling people that I understood how they felt because fighting and terrorist attacks were not a new thing in my country, but they didn't have a clue about the rest of the world. They just knew what was happening when it was happening to them and their own country. I found that really weird – I knew all the stuff that was happening in Moscow was on the news and on CNN so I guess I was just a little shocked that they didn't seem to know anything about it.

Of course, it was a very upsetting time for everyone in America. For a while the whole country was at a standstill and everyone was in mourning. You couldn't fly anywhere, security was completely tight, but people were so scared they didn't want to fly either. I did understand the tragedy of it all and when we travelled to New York six months later for a competition we went to see Ground Zero and it was a truly shocking sight. It had affected everyone in the States. It was in the news non-stop, constantly on TV, and for a while the whole country just stopped. By the beginning of October, flying internally in America was permitted, although of course the security was super-tight. Brian and I took part in a few small competitions and then in November we travelled to Ohio to take part in the second-biggest competition in the US after the Nationals, the Ohio Star Ball in Columbus.

This was where we made our 'big competition' debut and we danced the American smooth. Brian's parents Ron and Kathy flew in to watch and we competed in the Rising Star competition, which is when you make the transition from Amateur to Professional. And we did really well! We ended up fourth overall after about five heats, which was amazing for us, and so we were really, really happy.

Not only did we do well but we had been noticed, too. The judges and other dancers had started to talk about us – we had come onto the radar, as it were. It also helped that we were often out and about with Bob and Julia, spending time with them over that competition weekend. We felt privileged that we were their friends and people started realising we were like their protégés so it was good for us in other ways, too. It was also good to watch other couples competing and seeing different styles and meeting new people. I got quite friendly with lots of Russians who had come over from a dance school in New York. It was altogether a positive experience and good that we had come onto the scene and made people talk. And I think it helped that we were a good-looking couple, too – Brian was a very handsome boy and because I was a bleached blonde Russian girl, just like Julia, they all thought I was her sister to begin with. But I didn't mind that if it helped us get noticed!

We also had a good result in the Professional category that we entered and made it through to the semi-finals. To be part of the Top 12 couples was really encouraging.

To be fourth in the Rising Star category and make the semi-finals in the Professional category made people wonder where we had come from and I remember the audience stomping their feet and cheering for us after we had danced. It was a fantastic feeling but I also felt so overwhelmed: it was like this was my dream but it wasn't a dream any more!

I knew I had worked hard to get there; this was what I had always wanted to do and being watched and cheered on in an arena filled with about 5,000 people was just incredible. Not to mention how kind and sweet people were, too, coming up to us and congratulating us afterwards. It was exactly what we needed to happen – to believe that we had done the right thing as a couple, to think my move to America was worth it. Sadly, while all the admiration and acceptance were amazing, we quickly realised that if we wanted to actually start winning these sorts of competitions or certainly move up in the rankings, we would not only have to dance the dances, we'd have to play the game, too...

CHAPTER 12

Dancing to the right tune

As far as dance teachers were concerned, we had only worked with Bob and Julia and, while we trusted them and felt they were helping us enormously with our routines and choreography, they were of course still competing themselves. So people started asking us why we still wanted to be taught by a couple we might eventually end up competing against.

But we never saw it like that: we never thought we would stand a chance against them as they were the champions and all we wanted to do was learn from them. Then we found that some of the judges who were marking us in competitions were saying that we needed to think carefully about our mentors and they started dropping hints that it wouldn't be a good idea if we continued to use Bob and Julia. It was all getting quite political and it was at that point we realised that to be successful in this world, we would need to play the game, too.

Now at first this was difficult for me to understand. I had come from Russia with the understanding that if you work hard and put the effort in, you let the dancing speak for itself. But if we wanted to get anywhere in this business, it didn't seem that was how you progressed. I needed to speak to someone about what was expected of us so I asked Julia, who revealed some home truths about the ballroom dancing world.

'Unfortunately, Kristina, it isn't always the work you put in that will get you anywhere, it's about the judges and the couples they teach, that is how they make a living. They don't get much money from judging so they teach couples and then put those couples through the different rounds in competitions. It looks good on them and more couples then want to be taught by them,' she explained.

So the judges who adjudicate in the big competitions have dancers who they teach, who then make it to the final. But it didn't always work that way: Bob and Julia had been champions for many years and were loved throughout the dancing industry. There was no mistaking their ability either, so while on some level what Julia had told me made sense, you also had to have the talent to be champions like them.

There was another couple always running second to Bob and Julia, who some of the judges were really pushing to be champions, but when it came down to the marks, they just weren't as good. Yes, you can push them all you want but when it comes to crowning the champions, you have to give it to the ones who deserve it. Bob and Julia never let their standard of dance drop.

Brian and I were very proud people and we didn't want to get involved in all the politics and unspoken rules, so we decided that we would just let our dancing speak. If anything it made us more determined, so we continued as we were and we started entering more competitions. It did work for a while as I think people realised how much we loved dancing and how enthusiastic we were. New on the circuit, we were showing people how much we enjoyed what we were doing.

We did decide, however, to follow some advice that another couple had given us, which was to head to New York and seek out the teaching talents of Paul Killick. One of the most famous ballroom dancers in the world, he had been British champion for many years. 'If you want to up your game, head to New York and have a few lessons with Paul,' we were advised.

As a little girl back in Russia I grew up watching Paul Killick on videotape, right from the beginning when he was just an amateur to when he became a professional champion, so to even consider having a lesson with this man was unreal! Of course, Brian was adamant that if it was going to help us as a couple, money was no object and I was so, so excited! So we flew to New York where Paul was teaching at his friend's school and started our lessons with him. We loved every second. Paul was very good with technique, very strict but very positive, too. He said that Brian was special and just needed time to develop his technique and grow as a dancer and my strong Russian-taught techniques complemented him well.

Both of us really loved his lessons and soon became hooked. We also found that it really synced us as a couple, too. Obsessed with Paul and his partner Hannah, we started saving money to fly him to Seattle ourselves or we would save money to travel to England when he went back to the UK to compete. Paul was actually living in Kent and although we spent a fortune on seeing him, we were obsessed and basically made him our primary coach. We thought he was doing wonders for us as a couple and was therefore worth every penny.

But it soon became clear that we had upset quite a few people by this association and were getting their backs up. Word got around that we were taking lessons on dancing American Rhythm from someone from England. The American teachers and judges didn't like it and they made it quite clear that they felt snubbed. According to them, it was as if we were saying that they weren't good enough to teach us, that we had to go to England to be taught. It completely rubbed them up the wrong way. Of course, that wasn't the case at all, we had just found someone who worked for the both of us and who had eliminated the arguments we used to have about what needed to be done and how it must be done to make our performances better.

What was the problem with that?

We felt Paul was helping our performances so much that a year later, when we returned to the Emerald Ball championships in Los Angeles in May 2003, we won first place in the Rising Star category, which, for a couple who had been dancing together for just over a year, was quite unheard of. That cemented our relationship with Paul and we decided that he could help us go all the way to become National Champions. We didn't want to take lessons from anyone else and we started making it into the finals of the bigger competitions, too, coming fifth or fourth place and seeing that winning post within our grasp.

As a couple we wanted to succeed so badly – not only because Brian and his family had put a lot of faith in me in bringing me over to their country but also because we had worked really, really hard over the past two years. We lived and breathed dancing and there was nothing else in our lives more important – we were so driven, so young and in love. Yes, we were in love and had started dating at that point, too. When you are spending so much time with someone, living and breathing dancing, it is a very natural development to start dating your dance partner. It happens a great deal in this industry and when you are young and sharing the same goal in life, the same hobby and the same love for something, you think that is all it takes to have a good relationship. You are in a complete bubble: you don't go out to meet other people as you are always dancing and if you do go out and meet someone else, then you find you don't have any time to spend with that person as you are always rehearsing or competing. And then to top it all off, you are spending time travelling round the country and dancing with your partner – another man! So who would want to date you?

So yes, dancers do end up dating each other, but you will also find that they usually end up splitting once their professional careers are over. They realise that the thing that was gluing them together was the only thing they really had in common. But for Brian and I at that time, we were determined. Although the hours were brutal, in our minds there was no other way, as there was nothing more important to us than to succeed on the dance floor. And all our money was going into dancing. We might skip a lunch but we would use that money to pay for a lesson in the evening or to hire a studio to rehearse. We were lucky that we lived with his parents and could therefore put every single penny we earned through teaching into our dancing. Paying for Paul was expensive but he was a legend and so worth every penny.

But then the dancing mafia, as I like to call them, reared their ugly heads. A year after becoming Rising Star Champions and making regular appearances in the finals of most of the competitions we entered, suddenly we found ourselves dropping marks and not getting past the semi-finals stages. And then suddenly we were struggling to get through all the heats of the competitions, too. We couldn't understand what was happening – our standard hadn't dropped and we were certainly as committed as ever. And then it dawned on us: the judges weren't going to forgive us for not using them as our teachers. It was like some sort of grooming, I suppose. We would pick up on hints from some of the judges after our performances, like, 'Oh, you should come to one of my lessons… I could do this for you, I can make that happen for you, etc., etc.'

I remember being stopped by one of the judges after a big competition in which we had done particularly badly. He told us in no uncertain terms what the problem was. We were walking down the hotel corridor (a lot of the competitions were held in hotels with large ballrooms or function rooms for performances) and he stopped us both cold.

'So, guys, that wasn't a great result, was it? I think you need to start respecting the society you are in and we are all there to help you. Do you still want to take lessons overseas and still compete in our competitions? You are snubbing all of us! You think we're not good enough as teachers and you are travelling all the way to England to be trained. And you think we are actually going to let you win or get the title? Who do you think you are?'

So there it was, clear as day. Unless we started playing the game we weren't going to get anywhere. I suspect it happens in other sports but I know our world is especially cruel. When you have five or six judges watching your every move (with up to eleven in the bigger competitions) it does to a certain extent come down to their own personal opinion. There are so many aspects of your performance – technique, speed, chemistry, the artistic side – to judge that it sometimes feels as though it just comes down to personal preference. There is no Olympic measure in the world of dancing. If you run a race and you are the fastest and cross the finishing line first there is no denying you are the winner. Or if you jump the furthest or throw the furthest there is always a clear champion.

It was very apparent from that conversation that the judges were teaching us a lesson and that they were cross with us because for two years we never took a lesson with anyone from America. I suppose we had been a little naïve, too. We were young and hungry to succeed the right way, to let our dancing speak for itself. That was always what I was taught and Brian was also like that, and so when we started losing to couples who weren't as good as us but were connected, it was hard. It seemed like the judges didn't care about us at all, they were too busy marking up the couples who were taking lessons with them, bringing them business and earning them money. We felt like an outcast couple who no one cared for, and not a single judge would stand up for us. Bob and Julia didn't have any influence over the judges for us either. If anything, our association with them worked against us as I think they saw similarities in our routines and to be champions you couldn't copy anyone, you had to be unique, so I did understand that idea.

So we went back home and spoke to Brian's parents, who

were very supportive. They didn't really understand what was going on but they did say to us that it was our money and we had invested so much time and effort in our dancing already, why not take a couple of lessons with one or two of the judges and see what happened? We were devastated. I started to cry and was very upset with this harsh reality and it did put us in a horrible position. We began to argue and blame one another and, both being so young, it took us a while to accept that we would have to give in and play the game that was expected of us. But we hated the idea: not only did it feel like we were conforming to this underhand way of being successful, but we had to pay someone who we didn't think would actually help our dancing a great deal but who would have influence when it came to scoring and mark us favourably.

So we did what we had to do and it felt like we were selling our souls to the Devil. We knew that we were wasting a lot of money but we also accepted that in order to please those who ruled the world in our business, we had to be clever. So we decided that, OK, we would play by the rules but we also wanted to continue to work with Paul and not let our dancing suffer. But to be honest, the whole idea and reality of this was bringing us down as a couple. It broke our spirits and we were both unhappy and fighting loads with each other. That meant that we were still not seeing very good results at competitions because we weren't connecting at all well and therefore we were not enjoying ourselves.

While it's not unusual for dancing partners to start dating, equally when the dance stops it's not unusual for professional partners to split up. Suddenly there's nothing to say to each other and Brian and I found ourselves in a similar position.

Living in such a negative way, we broke each other's spirits. We felt that we had made so many sacrifices to do things the right way yet we were still struggling.

For us it was the beginning of the end, really.

CHAPTER 13

Dancing with the Stars? It will never work...

B rian and I decided to start competing again. We were
working with the judges, still working with Paul, and yet
we still weren't getting the marks we had hoped for. In fact,
we were still being marked below couples that we knew were
not as good as us and, while we understood that we weren't
going to get marked up straight away, it was hard. We started
to fight a lot and, as I have said, we weren't really connecting
as a couple.

Of course, every couple fights on the dance floor, whether
in a relationship or not, but we were married by that time and
living together. We got married in a very small and simple
ceremony as we didn't have a lot of money to spend on it. We
weren't having a great deal of time apart, it was very intense
and it wasn't a happy time in our dancing or relationship. Up
until that point we were happy – we worked hard and it was

tough but we were happy. Now I felt I needed to have my own space but because I didn't have my own car, I had to rely on Brian or his family for lifts, so it didn't ever really feel like I had time to breathe.

And buying a car meant not buying a dress for the next competition or not being able to afford to pay for travel for a lesson with Paul, so this was always the choice and dancing came first.

I was missing everyone at home, too, and I think Brian and I both started to feel that we wanted time away from each other. It was a vicious circle: we would compete, we would be upset with the result, and then we would start blaming each other. Of course it was very immature but we were only twenty-five years old at that time, we didn't know how to deal with this pressure and stress and cracks formed in our relationship.

The sad thing was we would fight while rehearsing and then we would fight when we came home and his parents would see us angry and upset. But then again that was another thing that annoyed me about the situation: Brian and his family were so close that there were no limits to what they talked about. For them it was all about communication – they would talk openly about everything. It was very hard as when we would argue in our room, for example, right away he would go out and be like, 'Mum, Dad, we need your advice…'

I would be really cross with him for that because I was embarrassed and I didn't think they should be involved in our fights. And I didn't want them to think I was ungrateful in any way. If Brian was unhappy it felt like it was all down to me and I was bringing unhappiness upon the whole family. But I was cross with Brian that we just couldn't sort it out ourselves. I never had that level of support from a parent; instead I buried so many of my problems and dealt with everything on my own because that was how I was able to survive. But Brian wasn't brought up to hide his feelings and I started resenting him for this. Of course, I now understand that is what family is for, to talk about things, but at the time it made me feel very uncomfortable and embarrassed.

As we were still struggling in competitions we started thinking maybe we ought to look for another coach. Lessons with Paul were helpful but he was still competing himself and it was hard to find time to get together. So we decided to look closer to home and as luck would have it, there was another famous dancer and teacher, Louis van Amstel, who had just moved from Holland to Salt Lake City in the US. He was known for his eccentricity and his unique style while performing and we were really keen to meet him and see if he could help us in any way.

So we arranged a lesson with Louis and it felt like he had breathed fresh air into our dancing again. He was a good coach and having retired only a couple of years ago, we felt he could really guide us on where to focus our energies. We would go to Salt Lake City and stay in his house and as we weren't the only dancers there either, it made us feel better. And we weren't the only ones struggling, which made us feel less isolated and negative about everything. With Louis' guidance we started doing competitions again and even though the judges still weren't marking us as high as we would have liked, I think there was a shift in how people were treating us. They began saying more positive things and I think the lessons with the judges did help as they appreciated that we were playing the game a little bit, too.

We had a bit of hope again!

While we were moving in the right direction for dancing, our relationship as a married couple was damaged, so in the end we just focused on being dance partners. We didn't enjoy just being us – going for a walk, or going out to a restaurant or maybe talking about something else other than dancing – it was always dancing, dancing, dancing. We were a team, we would fight for each other, and if anyone said anything negative about me or Brian, we would stick up for each other, but there was no love as a man and woman between us any more.

I did get a few people asking me why I was dancing with Brian and telling me that I could do so much better with this person or that person, but it was always a judge who would be trying to break us up. It is a cruel world in a sense and every coach wants to put a winning medal on their own chest saying, 'Look, this is my couple, I have made these two champions.' It gives them a status and then they get attention from other dancers who want to be taught by the best in the business, too.

But I would never leave Brian: he and his family had changed my life, they gave me an opportunity and I couldn't just leave him. But I can't lie, it was preying on my mind, especially as our relationship wasn't great and we were always fighting with each other. I am sure Brian felt the same. But we focused on our dancing and competing and slowly things did start to improve. Then something funny happened. I remember Louis ringing us when we were in LA. It was May 2005 and we were competing in one of the big events over there and he called while we were taking a stroll along Sunset Boulevard.

'Listen, guys, I have just been asked to cast some dancers for a new show coming up on TV. It is a show about professionals dancing with celebrities. I have been asked to cast all the dancers and wondered if you would be interested in doing it.'

Brian and I were intrigued but when we asked how much they were paying the dancers, it was something really low, like $500 a week. We would make that in a day teaching so that wasn't an incentive at all! Louis did try and persuade us that it would be more about the exposure and he told us that he was going to be the main choreographer on the show, too, so we knew we could all work well together. But we had just started to climb up again in the competitions and we still had our dream to be champions and so we said no. Besides, why would we want to move to LA and work on a TV show that we didn't even know would succeed?

It was of course *Dancing with the Stars*. The show was brought to the States a year after it was broadcast here in Britain as *Strictly Come Dancing*. The TV network ABC bought the format and brought it to the States and the first season was terrible: the ratings were bad, the dancers weren't getting good money and the celebrities weren't that great either. So Brian and I were quite happy at the time that we had made the right decision about the show and thankful we hadn't said yes to Louis. I didn't, in a million years, think it would go on to do so well!

Louis said he understood and for him it was the perfect thing to do – they do two seasons a year in the States as the series runs are a lot shorter than ours. When the second season came around, ABC thought they should revamp the show and put more money into it to get better celebrities. And then it really hit the big time. All of a sudden the dancers became celebrities in their own right and they started appearing on *Larry King Live* and all the other big talk shows in America. We were hanging out with Louis a lot, too, and we also had a lot of friends who we knew from the competing circuit on the show. Louis once invited us to a big ABC party and we went with the dancers from *Dancing with the Stars*. It was very surreal as we saw lots of celebrities from all the big ABC shows on at that time, like the cast of *Desperate Housewives* and many other famous actors and actresses. And Brian and I thought to ourselves, maybe we shouldn't have turned it down after all. The show was really positive for the whole ballroom dancing business – people were talking about dancing and watching the skill that was involved. It really boosted the whole sport and I remember when I first moved to America and told people I was a ballroom dancer, they didn't have a clue what I meant. I think a lot of people thought it was like ballet!

We knew we had made the right decision to turn it down, though, as we had invested so much in our dancing careers and we were so close to getting where we wanted to be in the competitions.

After being crowned National Champions thirteen times, Bob and Julia announced their retirement in 2003. It was very sad in a way but it did mean the field was opened up a little bit more, too. Now there was a big question mark over our heads about whether we could win that title and we put pressure on ourselves to train harder than ever.

There was one other couple that came into our divisions in competitions and we knew they held a great deal of influence over the judges and competition organisers. The male dancer owned and ran lots of dance studios around New York and was very well connected. He knew all the competition organisers and his studios were used by a lot of the dancers and teachers. Who were we compared to them? We were just a couple from Seattle, we didn't have any influence; we just worked hard. We found out fairly early on that although Bob and Julia had retired, becoming champions was still out of our reach – in fact, we were told by the judges themselves we shouldn't be too surprised or upset by this. The other couple had the upper hand in most of the competitions. It didn't put us off, though: we knew we might not win anything but we hoped that people would still see that we were trying to be the best.

It was naïve, I suppose – we had worked really hard and the reality was, we would never be champions. It had been six years since I had first moved to the States and we had invested a lot into our dancing and yes, however foolish it was, we did want to be the next champions. But there is always going to be politics, influence and bribery involved in the dance world and the realisation completely broke us. We were always just Brian and Kristina, the couple who wanted to dance, but it got to the point when we thought, why should we carry on? Especially as everyone was telling us, 'Do your best, guys, but you're not going to win.'

Around this time I decided to buy a car. It was a very old and very cheap Toyota Corolla and I bought it from a friend of my best friend Alex in Seattle. I needed to be my own person and have that freedom, but it did affect my relationship with Brian as it meant that we were definitely spending more time apart. Alex was the one who gave me some good advice about this: 'OK, you are both too young to be this unhappy. I know it's all about dancing and working but you have to enjoy your life, too,' she told me. And she was right, we were both young and we could be happy and I think I knew at that point that this was the end of us as a dancing couple. We were constantly fighting, we weren't happy at home or on the dance floor any more as we knew it was never going to end the way we wanted it to – as champions.

We still took part in competitions and we would hope that we would beat the other couple and, to be fair, we did get a lot of people who would come up to us afterwards and say, 'You should have won!' But we didn't, we always came second. We would get the biggest standing ovations and we still didn't win. That was a tough year as we felt that we were working so hard but it was all for nothing. I suppose reality hit us that we could continue as we were for years and years, put every penny we earned into dancing, carry on living with Brian's parents and where would it get us? We could do that for the next ten years or so and still have nothing to show for it.

After Bob and Julia retired we kept going for a year and made it to the Nationals in Miami in 2006. My mum had come over from Russia to support us and Brian's parents were there too, so it felt like we had everyone we needed around us. In my heart, I knew this was going to be the last competition I danced in. Defeated, I felt it was time to let go of the dream. I remember speaking to my mum before the competition started and I confessed my decision.

'In my heart of hearts, Mum, I can't do this any more. I can't do it to myself or to Brian any more. We make each other miserable, we have lost a little bit of ourselves in that race for first place and I don't want to be unhappy any more and I don't want him to be unhappy any more. Do you think I am making the right decision?'

120

And she said to me, 'Kristina, you are only twenty-seven years old, you can't live your life like this – you're basically not having a life! Besides competing, you are spending all the money you have on dancing and what do you have to show for it?' And she was right: I didn't have anything to my name apart from a broken old car, a few trophies and a couple of dance costumes. All of my pennies went towards the dance competitions and paying to make us the best dance couple ever.

So it was at the Nationals that I made the decision this was to be my last dance professionally. I would focus on teaching and earning money that way, which would at least give me enough money to buy a house or an apartment or something.

As it happened, the encouragement we received at the Nationals was overwhelming. Lots of people were coming up to us between the heats and saying, 'If you don't win tonight, it will be a tragedy because it is clearly your title.'

We got to the final and we joined the five other finalists on the dance floor as the judges announced the runners-up. 'In sixth place… In fifth place… In fourth place… In third place…' And then it was just us and the other couple from New York again. It was a familiar sight, we were used to getting this far and feeling a tiny bit of hope… And then they announced us as the runners-up. Well, the whole room erupted, they went absolutely crazy; they were stomping and cheering and I told Brian not to move because I wanted to soak it all in, to savour every last clap. If this was going to be my last competition I wanted to enjoy this final show of admiration and I could see how much people really appreciated us. It was quite funny because when they announced the New York couple as the winners they did get some applause but it was nothing compared to the ovation that we received.

And they did come up to us at the end and say, 'Well, we know who people wanted to win. You are amazing guys and we are honoured to dance with you on the same floor.' That was something special and it was kind of them to acknowledge us, but they were still the champions.

At the after-party we had so many people saying, 'You should have won, you should have won!' And you know what? I couldn't hear it any more; I was so over it. We flew back to Seattle and it was nice to take a bit of time out with my mum, who was staying in America for another couple of weeks. Normally we would take about three weeks off after the Nationals anyway so Brian had time to be with his mates and I had the chance to spend time with my mum and Alex.

Mum flew back to Russia at the end of September and a week later we started getting calls from Louis, asking us when we wanted to fit in some dancing lessons to prepare for the Ohio State Ball, which was coming up in November. Because Louis had his other commitments with *Dancing with the Stars* I think he wanted to get some dates sorted out. But instead of arranging everything, I didn't get back to him straight away. Brian wanted to know what was going on and why I wasn't arranging lessons with Louis so I told him it was now time to be honest with each other.

'I just don't see the point of this any more,' I confessed. 'Spending all my life and all my money on this. I don't want to spend another five years being second to a couple who even acknowledge themselves that they shouldn't be winning. I just don't see the point. I'm sorry, Brian.'

It was a heartbreaking conversation and although we had broken up personally a couple of years earlier, to face the prospect that we needed to split up completely was so, *so* hard. We both cried a lot and he ran out of my room but he couldn't really argue back as he knew it was true: we were both unhappy and it had come to the point where one of us had to be the one to say enough is enough. Then I told him I was packing my bags and going to stay with Alex for a little bit – I had to do this for both of us. I told Brian that life was too short to make each other unhappy. What was the point of carrying on like this?

But I was a lot tougher than Brian:his family were always there for him whereas I was used to making big decisions by myself and I think I was the stronger one of the couple. He tried to convince me that we should still compete together as we had people relying on us, but I was adamant that for once it was time to think about ourselves: 'The big dancing machine will keep going without us,' I said.

He knew I was right, but I still felt terrible. I needed to get out of the house as I couldn't look Kathy and Ron in the eye and I was so pleased that I could escape to Alex's place. So I packed my stuff and I left, leaving a letter for Kathy. Yes, it was a cowardly thing to do, but I didn't feel strong enough to have a conversation with her or Ron. I knew if I did, they would try and convince us to stay together. And I probably would have given in as they meant so much to me. I knew I would have felt pressured to somehow make it work just for them. So I wrote a letter to Kathy, explaining why I couldn't talk to them about it: I had made a decision and now I needed to be on my own for a little bit as I didn't want to be confused or influenced by anyone else.

But it was hard and I was crying my eyes out while I was

writing this. I wanted them to know how much I treasured them as they had taken me in as part of their family for the past six years. In a way, my grief over leaving Brian and the family wasn't really about the dancing; in my heart I had realised that it wasn't working for a while. I was more upset to think that I was leaving them, and all the things I loved about them. It felt like I was losing something that I had yearned for so much in my life: a family. But in a way I was using them too, to keep up a pretence of something that just wasn't working. And it wasn't right. I gave it my best shot, no one could argue with that, but I couldn't do it any longer.

The next few days were awful. I spent a lot of my time crying and I felt like I did all those years ago when I was twelve years old and had to leave my grandparents' flat.

I was alone again.

CHAPTER 14

Once a dancer, always a dancer...

A lex was very supportive and kind but it was a tough few months for me after walking out on Brian and his family. I had filed for divorce and it was done quickly a few months later. I started to question whether I had done the right thing: I felt like a failure for not having made it work dancing with Brian and we had lost a lot of work as I had to cancel engagements and shows that he and I had been booked on as a couple. There were still a few people whom I could teach, so I tried to concentrate on them. I wasn't interested in competing any more, although when word got round that Brian and I had split up, I had a lot of calls from potential partners, asking me to join them. But I would never do that to Brian. And I certainly didn't want to compete in the same division, American Rhythm, with anyone else because he and I had got so far in that category and it wouldn't feel right dancing with someone else.

I remember getting a phone call from one of our teachers with whom we occasionally took lessons. He told me about a guy who was looking for a partner just to do shows with, not to compete with. The shows were mostly in Asia and Japan and basically that meant travelling to dance schools to perform in their summer or Christmas balls, or if they were putting on an event and they needed a few couples to keep the audience entertained. Michael, the dancer in question, had been retired for four years but he had heard I was now solo and he wanted to meet me. It seemed like a good idea as I didn't want to compete either, and just doing the shows would give me a little income too, which would help.

In his amateur days Michael had been a world champion and then he turned professional and was ranked third or fourth in the world in the International Professional Latin division, the style I danced a lot back in Russia. He was an incredible dancer, it was my dream to dance with someone like him – he was the level of Paul Killick. To be honest, I couldn't believe he wanted to try-out with me. Michael had a lot of followers in Japan and ballroom dancing was quite big in Asia on the whole; it was a very big part of their culture. Why was that? I think it was partly because they would suppress their emotions in day-to-day life so dance was a way they could express themselves openly.

In a way it was strange for me to think I could be going back to Japan – it was where I was competing as a teenager. I didn't actually think the partnership with Michael would work out as I knew there were lots of other girls who wanted to dance with him, but I thought to myself, why not? I'll have a go. So the coach that contacted me organised a try-out and I went to meet him. In fact, we had crossed paths before at the bigger competitions and although we were in different divisions we had quite a few mutual friends on the circuit, so he knew of me. We had a try-out and we found that we really liked dancing together – which for me was like a dream come true!

I was very different from his previous dancer, a lot more showcase, a lot more emotional on the dance floor and a lot more theatrical. That was perfect for Michael as the shows were about just that – putting on a great show. It was funny, he told me later, he had convinced himself that he just wanted to retire and do a bit of judging and teaching and didn't think anything would come from meeting me – he just thought it would be good to see if there was any show spirit left in him. But once we started to dance he knew show dancing still excited him and he was very enthusiastic about it all again.

At the time, he was thirty-four years old and I was twenty-seven and we decided just to go for it. He had lined up a couple of weeks of shows in Japan and he told me, 'Let's have a go and see what happens.' So we put a few routines together and I was learning a lot from him, plus I was dancing a style I had been dancing in Russia, so in a way it was like I was going back to my roots. We visited Japan several times and I enjoyed dancing with him so much. They loved Michael and he had a very loyal fan base, which meant I received a warm welcome as his partner, too.

We went there for Christmas at first. I had split up with Brian only a few months earlier, so we didn't have long to put our show together but I absolutely loved it. Of course there was a lot of pressure, too: I was going on the floor with one of the best dancers in the world and nobody knew who I was, so I had to make sure I stood out. But I did say to myself I just needed to relax and enjoy it, think about the little bit of money I could make and then see where it took me.

It turned out that I ended up working for a couple of years with Michael because we established a good name for ourselves in Japan as a very entertaining couple – our shows were quite unusual and very theatrical and people loved them. I enjoyed creative choreography and we produced a really good showcase. We started getting booked all over the world – Japan, Taiwan, Argentina, South Africa – we were all over the place! I think it must have been about a year into our performing as a couple when we both started to get the buzz to compete again. Certainly, I think Michael was beginning to think in the back of his mind, 'OK, what if?' It's that fire inside of you, it doesn't ever go, and I was eager, too – we were popular as a couple, we were dancing well together, maybe we should.

So we entered a few little competitions in America, nothing that put too much pressure on us, and we did well; it made us feel good. And then we ended up competing in the biggest competition in the world, The British Open Championships at The Blackpool Winter Gardens. Everyone in our world knows that the British Championships is the biggest competition in our business. It is open to the world, which means anyone can compete and anyone can come – it's a big international competition. I had competed there with Brian and had studied a style called Theatre Art, which is like a showcase with lots of lifts and tricks and a lot like Cirque du Soleil – it's called 'showcase' or 'theatre art' division. Brian and I did this for a couple of years and we got an invite to represent America in this style in Blackpool in 2004 and came second, which was amazing.

My whole association with Blackpool was quite special and competing there with Brian was a great honour, so I thought to myself, 'Wouldn't it be amazing to compete at an international level here with Michael?' We were dancing well together and we both felt hungry for competing again, me especially. I felt that I still had a lot to give and, as I was dancing with one of the best dancers in the world, I'm not afraid to admit that the competitive edge did come out in me again. So we made the decision to go and it was an interesting year as there were a lot of couples like us who had split up, gone off and done their own thing with other partners and now decided to come back and compete again.

When you go to a big competition like that with a new partner you have to start at the very beginning again, which means you have to work your way through heats. I think we danced in five heats before reaching the semi-final and because of the number of couples you have to do all your dances in each heat. So you have to be so fit, physically, as all the dances are high speed or very intense and each dance is two and a half minutes long. Then you have a twenty-minute break before you go to the next heat. It's very full-on and if you progress through the competition, you make it to the semi-final but you are so exhausted! At that stage you have to be able to dance your absolute best so you can't be tired. You see couples who give it their all in the first couple of heats and who are physically strong but by the third or fourth round they start falling apart as they haven't worked on their endurance; the quality of the dancing completely falls apart.

I learnt a lot from Michael during that time, your adrenaline gets you through a lot and Blackpool is an amazing place.

And when you are being judged by the best of the best in your sport, there is no way you can back off or feel tired, you just have to deliver. In the end we made it to the semi-finals. We danced with the top twelve in the world in the professional division and that feeling of competing with the cream of the crop was incredible. There was no feeling of tiredness, I just felt so happy that we had made it to the semi-finals. That was good enough for me but not for Michael: he was used to competing in finals and having been in the top three in the world before he retired, it wasn't a good result for him. Everyone said it was quite an achievement to get that far with me – a girl that no one really knew – especially as we hadn't been competing in any small competitions in the UK, so there wasn't really a chance for people to warm to us. It was an amazing result but it was hard for Michael and I understood that. It didn't make him happy. He had that competing bug again and wanted to do well and while for me it was all exciting and new, I think he regretted coming back and not doing as well as he had done previously.

Immediately after Blackpool we went back to America to rehearse for some more shows in Japan and that trip was hard for us as mentally we were in different places. I felt ecstatic to have reached the top twelve in the world whereas he was disappointed and perhaps kicking himself for daring to compete again.

It wasn't hard to see that this partnership wasn't going to get us anywhere – I couldn't force him to compete and I didn't want to go to Japan any more and spend months just dancing in shows, so I actually said to him it was time for us to go our separate ways. I had had the best deal out of our partnership as I had learnt so much from him and he made me the dancer I am now. In those two years I made massive leaps in my level of dancing and technique; I had danced and competed with the best of the best in the world. Other than Blackpool, the highlight of my time was the summer of 2007 when Prince Mikasa of Japan asked us to perform for him at his Summer Ball in Tokyo. It was incredible and I was so very grateful for that experience with Michael. I knew I was lucky that he chose me to dance with him in the shows. And after two years of travelling all over the world taking part in the shows, we both felt it was time to settle down. I wanted to go back to America and organise my life, and he wanted to go home to South Africa. We parted as friends.

So I went back to the States with a mind to get my judging licence and then continue to teach and judge competitions. By then I was twenty-nine years old and I thought I had made more of a name for myself. OK, so maybe I was just one of a long line of girls who had danced with Michael, but it was a fantastic chapter in my life and it felt like the right ending to my experience as a competitor. I moved from Alex's home in Seattle to LA as *Dancing with the Stars* was getting bigger and more popular. It made sense to be nearby, where I might be able to pick up work either teaching or judging. I took my judging exams and got my licence to judge but I still felt a little bit at a standstill: I could judge when I was sixty-nine, but I was only twenty-nine… Was I giving up too early?

Then Louis van Amstel came back into my life. He rang me and said, 'I've heard you've split up with Michael. I have some news – *Dancing with the Stars* are putting together a live tour around the country, a winter tour and a summer tour. I am a choreographer on the tour and I need company dancers to take part alongside the other professionals and celebrities. I need two boys and two girls and I wondered if you would like to be one of the girls?'

He went on to explain that I would get a decent pay. I would travel around the US for about two months at a time and it would give me a bit of insider experience to see if I would ever want to be on the show. That is what a lot of people in my industry now wanted to do, to get on *Dancing with the Stars*, and Louis said it would help give me an idea about how I felt about the TV world.

So I rented a little place in LA and I asked my mum to come and live with me. I was lonely and the lifestyle of a dancer means you never really settle, as quite often you are travelling all over the place. And I did think it would be nice to have Mum around and we could live together for a while. I also needed her support – I wanted to come home and find my mum there. So she rented out our flat in Vladivostok for six months, packed her bags and came over to live with me.

I went on the *Dancing with the Stars* tour and it was a great experience. I learnt a lot about the world of TV and I knew a lot of the professional dancers as I had seen them only a few years ago competing on the circuit. I remember saying to Louis that I couldn't believe how much they had changed, though – TV seemed to have affected them. Most of them were OK with me, but they were constantly craving attention and wanting to be famous, which made them a little wary of new dancers coming into their world and possibly taking any attention away from them.

But I didn't really find it appealing at all, the fame – it seemed to be a very weird world. I saw the show as a way of making money out of something I loved to do so I could support my family. There were a couple of girls on the show who had been on it for a few years and they were getting a lot of attention because one was always splitting up with her boyfriend and then getting back together, while the other one had had a big row with her celebrity and his family and it was in the press so much at the time. It seemed horrific to me. I couldn't believe that they could be happy living their lives with the paparazzi chasing them the whole time and wanting to know all about their private lives. Little did I realise the press attention I myself would be dealing with just a few years later.

The tour was fun, though – I was dancing again and I really enjoyed it. And the funniest thing was that the opening night was in Seattle of all places! Over the past couple of years I had started to reconnect with Brian's parents. I knew that I wasn't ever really going to have a particularly good relationship with Brian again as he would be dating someone else and I didn't want to be the annoying one popping up from the past. But for me it was so important to try and reconnect with his family – I wanted them to understand how much I loved them as my second family. At Christmastime I would send them presents and after visiting Japan with Michael, I invited them all out to dinner and we had a good chat and a good time together. I think they understood why I had done what I did, but I wanted them to realise just how much they meant to me.

Time is a great healer and when I started to dance with Michael I heard that Brian had found another dance partner, too, so I felt life had moved forward for both of us. The whole family had had time to move on; they understood that whatever happened between Brian and me, life goes on. They didn't make me feel bad for leaving and I will always be grateful for that. So I kept in contact and when I moved to LA and heard the opening night was in Seattle, I invited them to come and watch me in the show. Brian didn't come – for whatever reason – but I was grateful that Kathy, Ron and Sean came and we went out for dinner afterwards. I think they were proud of me. They had given me that chance, in bringing me to America, and now they were watching me in the *Dancing with the Stars* tour and I was so pleased that we had managed to repair our relationship.

It was a long tour around the States; we performed in every city possible. We started at the beginning of December 2007, and we were only allowed a few days off at Christmas and New Year. One of the celebrities on the tour was Wayne Newton, also nicknamed 'Mr Las Vegas', who was quite a famous guy in America. A fantastic singer and entertainer, for over thirty years he had a one-man show in Vegas. The night before New Year's Eve we had a tour show in Vegas and then, as we had a couple of days off before leaving Nevada, he invited the whole cast to come and celebrate New Year's Eve and enjoy a big lunch and a horse parade at his ranch, just outside Vegas. The place was huge and he had lots of horses and horse-riding stables.

It was pretty incredible to be in his house as it was filled with all this amazing artwork and memorabilia, like signed photos of him and Elvis Presley. It was absolutely fascinating! He had a little girl, Lauren, and she and his wife Kathleen would come to the shows to see us, too. His wife once asked if I would give Lauren a couple of dance lessons – she loved watching us all dancing. So I taught her a couple of steps from one of the dances and Lauren's mum was really touched that I had taken the time to give her daughter a lesson. She gave me more of a personal tour of the ranch and talked to me about what it meant to be in the celebrity environment. I was talking to them like they were a normal family but Wayne was such a mega, mega star and it did make me think, 'Wow, what a fantastic place this show-business world is!' I loved the idea of it all, and it made me realise at that point that taking part in the main show, *Dancing with the Stars*, was something I now wanted to do.

So when we left Vegas and went back on the tour bus I was sitting with Brian Fortuna, who was in the dancing cast of the main show, and we were talking to one of the producers from the tour. He was a British producer who had been sent over from the UK show, *Strictly Come Dancing*, to look after the US tour. His name was Guy Phillips and he was a lovely person so I felt that I could talk to him quite openly about my desire to join *DWTS*. I asked him if I could take a screen test for the next series and he was very tactful about explaining that, although he thought I was an amazing dancer and he could see how much I enjoyed being on the tour, he didn't think the American show would take me on as they already had three Eastern European girls on the show. But then he told me he knew that *Strictly Come Dancing* were looking for another professional couple to take part as they wanted to increase the number of celebrity dancers involved from fourteen to sixteen for the next series. Therefore they needed one more male and female professional dancer to partner the extra celebrities. Brian Fortuna was really excited and straight away told me he was going to try-out for the part of male dancer, but all I could say to him was, 'But I live here, I don't want to live in England!'

It was a gut reaction as it felt like I had already changed my life once fairly drastically by moving to the States from Russia. Of course it wasn't that I had anything against England, but it seemed like another big jump for me. And I had asked my mum to come over from Russia to live with me in LA and had just started renting my own flat, so I really wasn't sure if this was a good opportunity or not. Guy explained that the series of *Strictly* was only four months long, so I wouldn't have to be in the UK forever if I didn't want to, and once I had done the show, I could return to America. And who knows, having *Strictly Come Dancing* on my CV might work in my favour when it came to taking part in *Dancing with the Stars*.

I really appreciated Guy's advice and he put me in contact with the producers of *Strictly Come Dancing* and I received an email asking me to send in all my showreels and CV, etc. It was the middle of January 2008 and they explained they were finishing their auditions for that year's show on 15 February, so if I did want to be considered for *Strictly* I would have to come and audition on that day. It was all a little crazy and it worked out that Brian and I would finish our last show for *Dancing with the Stars* in Philadelphia, then we would have to fly directly to London to do the screen test.

Brian was really keen to go and he persuaded me that it was too good a chance to miss. His enthusiasm was infectious. If we got the job we would be dancing the professional group dances with each other and I did feel comfortable dancing with him, so I just thought, 'Yeah, why not?'

So we flew to London, went straight to the BBC and met one of the producers. We had a forty-minute interview on camera – everything was being filmed for the executive producer to watch later – and it felt like it went on for ever. She was asking us a lot about what our teaching methods might be like – 'What would you do if your person isn't very good?' and 'What would you do if the person you are teaching is very difficult or has a temper?' The list seemed endless but I gave them very honest answers and explained that I had studied psychology in college so I felt prepared for working with different personalities. I had also worked with so many different pupils in America who had a varying range of abilities and I knew I could work just as well with a complete novice as with someone who had a little dance background. And I had been teaching young children since I was fourteen years old in Russia so it wasn't something I was worried about. I told them I loved choreography and I loved doing interesting, new and exciting stuff on the dance floor.

Then they asked Brian and I to perform a routine together so we did the cha-cha-cha, a routine that we had performed together on the *DWTS* tour. After that they asked me to actually show them how I would teach. They got one of the runners from the show who had never danced before and filmed me teaching him a few steps from the waltz and then the cha-cha-cha. Everyone was watching and then Brian had to do the same thing with a female runner and then all they said to us was, 'OK, guys, thanks very much. We'll keep in touch and let you know our decision soon.'

So we walked out after two hours of being in there and I turned to Brian and said, 'There is no way I will have got that job, why would they take me when they probably have hundreds of girls wanting that job and I am just a girl from Russia with a heavy accent that they probably couldn't even understand?' I didn't think for one moment that I would get the job.

But Brian just turned round to me and said, 'Kris, we've definitely got it!'

I had no idea why he thought that or why he was so confident that we would get the job – it was so funny the way he just said, 'Kris, we've definitely got it!' Maybe it was his edge of American cockiness, but he did think we did a good job in the interview and we were the characters that the show was looking for.

So we went back to our hotel, where only a few hours earlier we had dumped our bags, gathered them back up again and flew back to America. We were in London for just one day as there was no point staying any longer, and I really wanted to get home to see my mum. I hadn't seen her for ages as I'd been on tour, so it was nice to think when we got back to America, I could see her and take a bit of a break.

One of the first things I said to Mum when I got back was there was no way I would get the job on the show, so I needed to concentrate on teaching for a bit. And that was exactly what I focused on. I felt positive about it all, I wasn't dwelling on losing out on the show – I truly believed that I wasn't going to be offered a job. But I was living in LA and if ever there was a call from *Dancing with the Stars*, I was available. Plus, I also had my judging licence and I would have been happy to move around America if any judging opportunities came up. That is how I saw the next few months of my life.

I had absolutely no idea that the phone was about to ring and my life was going to take a whole new direction…

CHAPTER 15

Lights, camera, action!

It was a warm sunny day in May 2008 when I received the call. Being in London for twenty-four hours for a whirlwind audition back in February was a distant memory as I soaked up the LA sun. And then my phone rang and it was the producers from the show and I just heard the words, 'You've got the job!'

I was in total shock. I couldn't believe they wanted me as one of their professional dancers. Before I could even speak they carried on, explaining that I would have to come to London from August as the show runs from September to December. There were so many things to get organised too, and not only did they have to start processing my visa, I had to send them lots of information about all the competitions I had done, all my background – everything.

My mum couldn't believe it. She was so funny and said,

'Kristina, I have just moved from Russia to American to be here with you. And now you are leaving me!'

It was all a little bit surreal. My life was changing and moving in a totally new direction and I had no idea about what to expect – about the show or being on TV. In my mind, I saw it as just a job: I would make a bit of money, stay in England for four months and then come back to America. I never, ever thought I would stay in England more than I had to because I was happy in the States. After all, I had lived there for seven years and my life was very organised and settled and that is what I liked.

Of course I felt guilty about leaving my mum, even though she took it all in good spirits. When she first came over to America I arranged for her to start a course at the local college to study English as a second language. It was a six-month course and she was studying again (I have never known anyone enjoy learning as much as she does). I got friendly with a few ladies who I had taught and as they were slightly older, my mum's age, I encouraged Mum to meet them, too, and they started taking her out for coffee and things. That was really good for my mum as she felt that she was a little independent and had a couple of her own friends to talk to as well. But it was hard for her, too, as she was worried about me leaving for a whole new country again, so we tried to spend as much time together as we could in June and July.

We loved being in California together; it was by the sea, which made us both feel at home, and we really relaxed. Mum confessed that she had really, really missed me and had been very lonely. It was why she was so desperate to rent out the flat in Vladivostok to come and live with me in America. We both felt that we needed a home together, a base. Due to all the travelling I did with Brian and then Michael, it didn't really feel like I had a place I could call home for a long time. But now we were together and we did have somewhere to come back to each day. Was I really ready to leave it all for a new start in London?

I wanted to make my mum happy and I wanted to take care of her and that time together was very special as it was a good chance to rebuild our relationship, too. You can't choose your family and I understood that my relationship with my father was at a point where there wasn't much I could do to repair or rebuild it. I wasn't missing him and I didn't need him – does that sound sad? It was different when I was a child; I missed him a lot when he would disappear for weeks on end. But then that feeling was replaced with a lot of sadness and anger about the fact that he didn't help Mum when she needed him and he left me, a child myself, to deal with the difficult situation on my own. There wasn't anything more I could give to my relationship with my dad but it was important that I had my mum in my life and so I focused on that.

I can tell my mum anything now. If I'm scared, for example, which is something I never admit to anyone, or if I feel vulnerable. Sometimes I am very insecure – I have only ever really had myself to rely on, it was just me to question every decision and wonder if it was the right thing to do. That is a lot of pressure and there were many times when I had to make big decisions on my own when other people might have called their parents or siblings for advice. I learnt to make these decisions myself and trust my instincts, which made me a strong person.

In my gut, the decision to move to England for *Strictly* seemed like the right one. It was an adventure and, although I hadn't done TV work before, I had been teaching and competing for years now so I wasn't afraid of the actual work involved. Brian, who had been on *Dancing with the Stars*, told me that the TV industry was a whole different world and I would become more well-known – even if I was only on the show for one series. It was a stable amount of work, too, from August to December, and I would be earning a good wage, so it would benefit both my mum and me.

Was I excited at that point about being on television? To be honest I didn't know any different – I didn't know what it would be like or how my life would change. At that stage the only real excitement I felt was about the fact that I would be having a new adventure. I would be doing a new job and meeting new people and it made me feel alive again. After stopping my professional competing career I did think that maybe I wouldn't get the chance to dance again, although I was happy being a judge and a teacher. But I was only twenty-nine years old, so I still had that urge to dance within me.

It was another big move to a country where I wouldn't know a soul, though. I told myself I had done it before so I could do it again. There were dancers on the show that I had seen at competitions and recognised, but I didn't know them well enough to call any of them friends. It was good to go with Brian and have his support and advice.

So I had another tearful goodbye with my mum at the airport, but at least this time I knew that it would only be for a certain length of time and I was going over for a job, rather than moving to America with just a dream. When we landed in London, my first priority was to find a flat to rent as that was up to us to sort out ourselves. Part of the contract was that you had to be based in London for training so we knew we had to find something pretty quickly unless we wanted to waste all our money on hotels. But London was so expensive! I knew I didn't want the flat to be too far from the BBC and so I concentrated on the area around there, just trying to find something that wasn't too expensive to rent for my four-month stay. Brian wanted to have a luxury apartment and spend money on feeling comfortable and having somewhere nice to stay, whereas I felt completely differently and had the attitude of 'I am only going to be living here for a few months, I don't need a big space or anything fancy'. As a result I found the tiniest, tiniest little basement flat near Marble Arch tube station. It didn't have any windows in the walls because of it being in the lower basement and you would walk through the front door and fall into the bed because there was so little space! There was one kitchen unit on the side and it had a shower and a toilet. But it was cheap and I knew I could live there – I didn't want to spend a lot of money, I wanted to save as much as I could. Anyway, I had a nice flat in LA and I needed to support my mum: that was the priority.

I didn't ever invite anyone around because there was no space – you would struggle to turn around from the kitchen to the bed! But it was a good location, a few minutes' walk from the station, so it worked for me.

It wasn't long before the BBC got in touch saying they needed the dancers to be in the studio to start recording their interviews, profile pieces on TV and to begin doing photo-shoots. It was all very exciting, going to the BBC to have your hair and make-up done professionally, and people would be trying different costumes on us, too. I did my first profile shoot where I had to talk about myself and I just didn't have a clue what to say! It was very odd to stand in front of a camera and talk about myself, but Brian suggested I talk about the titles I had won, where I was from and what I enjoyed doing. It was good advice but still all very strange.

And then it was time to meet the celebrities. I don't know how familiar you might be with the show's format now, but back in 2008, my first series, it was a very different set-up. Today you get paired with your celebrity on what is called 'the launch show' and you have no idea who that is going to be until it is announced in front of the cameras. Back then it was up to you to travel with a TV crew in tow to meet your celebrity at a venue near them.

I remember getting in the car and being taken to meet my celebrity. The whole way there I was thinking to myself, 'This is so exciting! It's going to be someone really young and cool and hot. I'm ready to go, and ready to show off some fabulous routines with my young partner and really impress everyone!'

I got a phone call while I was in the back of the car from a dancer friend who I had met through Paul Killick, who was living in London. He rang to wish me luck and told me that he had been reading in all the newspapers that a singer called Peter Andre was the hot favourite to be taking part in the show and maybe I would be partnered with him. At the time, I had absolutely no idea who Peter Andre was, but according to my friend he was really famous and married to a famous model. I didn't have a clue – no disrespect to Peter Andre, I didn't actually know any UK celebrities – but I did think at that point, 'Great, he's famous and so lots of people will want him to do well!'

Then when we arrived at the building where I now thought Peter Andre would be, one of the producers took me to one side and said, 'Kristina, I just want to let you know that the person you are partnered with is a gentleman we have wanted on the show for years and years. We have been asking him for a long time and he's always refused, but he's finally said yes and we are so excited. So we are trusting you with this very important person. He is a national treasure and we are hoping you will be excited about working with him, too.'

Well, I was so pumped up after hearing that! I couldn't wait… Anyway, the camera crew were right behind me ready to start filming and all I had to do was walk into a room and formally meet my celebrity dance partner. I was all ready, all prepared, so excited, I opened the door… and on the sofa the lovely John Sergeant was seated.

Of course, at that time I didn't know how lovely he was. I just remember thinking, 'I don't know who this is, is this another producer from the show? Is he an agent of my celebrity?' And then he got up and came over and introduced himself to me. One of the first things he said was, 'I hope you aren't disappointed. I don't know anything about dancing but I will be listening to you and trying my best.'

I just remember staring at him, thinking, 'How on earth is he going to dance?'

He didn't look in any kind of shape to dance – where was my young, fit dance partner? I was a little in shock. I kept thinking, 'Why would they pair me with an older guy?' I had just finished

145

my competitive career so I could dance with someone younger and fitter and we could go all the way.

The most random thoughts kept popping into my head. I didn't really know what to say to poor John!

We had to have a chat while they filmed us and he was so sweet. He told me that he knew a little bit of Russian as his mother and grandmother were from Ukraine and he had visited Russia a fair few times so he knew all about my country and the culture and then he said, 'I hope you enjoy working with me.' It was so sweet. But then he told me that he had just been to the doctor as his feet were very swollen from walking a lot and that we would have to take lots of breaks from dancing as they were constantly swollen. At that point I couldn't hide my reaction.

'Oh my Lord, what am I going to do with you?' I exclaimed.

In my mind I was thinking, 'If he can't even walk because his feet will get swollen, how will he be able to dance?'

But he was so charming and I found myself laughing all the time because he was such a funny and sweet gentleman. When it came to being photographed in costume for the show we all met at the BBC and it was a chance to see who had been paired with whom and who the other celebrities were. I was coming up the stairs from the make-up room when I saw a couple of the professional male dancers and one of them said, 'Kristina, I'm so sorry! John was probably not what you hoped for and I hope you aren't too disappointed.'

But I just replied, 'I think I'll be OK!'

I didn't want to say I was disappointed because I certainly didn't want to sound ungrateful. The truth is, anyone can do well if they are young or fit or strong, but it is much more difficult to put your stamp on the show if you are the opposite

– and John was the opposite to all of that! Anyway, I went home that evening and googled 'John Sergeant'. I discovered that he was a very well liked political journalist who had been hit by the female British Prime Minister with her handbag. And at that point I thought to myself, 'You know what? I am going to try my hardest to do my best with him.'

I was very touched that he had thought the Russian connection would be something I would be interested in, and although he didn't try to speak any Russian to me – he only knew a few words – he knew a lot about my country. I can't really explain but it was very comforting being around him. I think I knew from that very first meeting that he was going to be good for me as he had a nice vibe and a very protective presence. And OK, he might not be that good a dancer, but already I could see he was going to be a kind person to work with.

So we started our first rehearsal. I remember it was a Thursday and I was told that our first dance together was going to be a waltz. I had to submit my song, which was Norah Jones' 'Come Away With Me', which is still my favourite waltz music. We started to rehearse and it was clear to me very early on that he was getting out of breath quite easily and we had to keep taking breaks as his feet were getting swollen. He would have to sit and do these foot exercises that his doctor had given him. A sixty-four-year-old man, he was overweight and out of shape and I knew I needed to be careful, but we had such a nice vibe going, we were always laughing. It was like dancing with my grandad – he was so sweet and always telling jokes.

Then the press got hold of the fact that John was taking part and dancing with me, the new Russian girl, and we spent a lot of time looking through the newspapers and laughing at the stories that had been written about us – complete polar opposites! He tried to explain his world of journalism to me and what the industry was like, and he did say he would try and help me out as much as possible with the press to protect me or raise my profile.

'Every interview I do on TV or with the newspapers, I will try to bring you along, too, so you get to know this world but you get to know it with me,' he said. It was so nice of him, I didn't expect such kindness – something that I was later to discover was quite rare in the world of TV and media.

He took me along to a photo shoot with one of his friends from the *Daily Mail* and he said I needed to be in my ballroom gown. It was the first interview I gave under John's supervision. I had no idea what the British press was like at that time – that was yet to come – so I was still quite naïve and I didn't know what I was doing. We were given no media training by the show and it was all so new to me. That first interview I did was nice and polite and looked fine in print and it was a positive piece.

After that, John took me to a few radio chat shows and TV shows – we were on the BBC's *The One Show*, for example. He was getting lots of interview requests but he always said he would only do it if I could go with him. I really appreciated that and he was very protective of me. I will always be grateful for that as he really cared and he really wanted to give me a glimpse into his world of journalism, but with his guidance. At the beginning you weren't allowed to have publicists or agents; every interview was done through the BBC press office and the dancers were forbidden to give interviews or talk about the show unless it was through the BBC, who would check the questions or sit in on the interviews.

I asked John what made him finally agree to take part in the show as they had been asking him for many years. He told me that he kept turning it down because he knew he was unfit and he wouldn't find it very comfortable. And then he thought it was rude not to take part after being asked so often!

'Kristina, I have everything I want in my life right now, I couldn't want any more,' he told me. 'I'm sixty-four and I have done lots of great things and have a one-man show and am doing comedy. There isn't anything I want from the show, I just want to have a good time and have fun. And who knows, I might learn a bit of dancing! I know I can't dance but I don't have anything to prove either.'

Every year since John and I were partnered together I have asked my celebrity dance partner why they decided to take part in the show. It is something I need to know right from the beginning, and some people say it's because they want to do well and learn a new skill and go all the way, while others want a bit of publicity and exposure – there are lots of different reasons. John's reason was just to have a good time and it made me feel a lot less stressed about it all. Before I knew I was partnered with him I did feel a lot of pressure that my choreography had to be amazing and my routines must be entertaining for the TV audience. Not only that, they had to be routines that I would be able to teach, too. But with John, I felt the important thing was for him to have a good time. He is who he is, and so I just had to make our dances as comfortable and easy as possible for him.

So I started putting a routine together, and it was fairly early on in our three-week preparations to learn the waltz that I realised he might be old but he had a very busy life! He had a lot of engagements and he was away on some kind of trip for one thing or another. And because he was performing his one-man shows, I had to travel with him, too – I remember visiting Cornwall for a day with him. I wanted to use every chance we got to rehearse and so I decided to use the theatre stage where he would do his show later that evening as a place to practise the waltz. But when we got to the theatre that morning it was all locked up so, while we waited for someone to come and open up, I suggested we could have a little practise outside – it was a nice warm day and we had the space. We thought nothing of it until the next day when there were pictures in the press of us dancing outside with a story that claimed John was worried about the show and trying to dance anywhere and everywhere he could to practise!

It made me laugh at the time. I could not understand why this was a story that was in the newspapers as we were just rehearsing. What was the big deal? I stayed for his one-man show that evening and loved it. He was such a brilliant presenter and had great comic timing, too. At one point he very kindly called me up on stage and introduced me to the audience, which was sweet of him.

So we had two weeks of training and that was when the stress really hit me. We were now in the studio rehearsing for the live show and I kept saying, 'Oh my goodness, it is a live show, anything could happen!'

I kept telling myself that I was being ridiculous and that I had danced in front of live audiences hundreds of times before, but the difference this time was that it was also on TV. It made everything a lot scarier. My biggest worry was that John would forget some steps as sometimes he would mix them up and I just wanted him to do well – it was such a lovely dance we had put together.

Of course, Brian had done the show in America so he knew what it was like, but I really was the new girl. Darren Bennett and Lilia Kopylova were also on the show and I knew her from various competitions and they were very kind and nice to me, as were Matthew Cutler and Ian Waite. They all tried to be supportive and helpful and reassure me.

You do feel quite supportive in one sense and you always wish the other *Strictly* couples well, but sometimes you are so focused on your celebrity, you can't think about anyone else. I remember standing behind the curtain and I heard the presenter Bruce Forsyth call out, 'Dancing next, John Sergeant and his dance partner, Kristina Rihanoff!', and I just felt like my heart was going to explode. I was so petrified! But John had sensed how tense I was and so he just squeezed my hands and smiled at me. He wasn't nervous at all! Out of all the celebrities I have worked with, and having been on the show for seven years, he was the only one who didn't ever seem nervous. It was a comfort as it reminded me what the show was all about for him – he just wanted to have some fun and to have a good time. And at that moment, I knew whatever would be, would be, although it felt like a bit of a role reversal as he led me out onto the dance floor.

I started dancing and my training kicked in as soon as I sensed him wobbling over some steps. And so I guided him and kept him going, and he did a lovely waltz as his first dance. The judges gave us OK marks but it didn't count towards anything as it was the first week and no one was voted off. They said it was very sweet and endearing, and I was very proud of him. At the end of the day it was his world he was taking me into, in a sense. Although I was the one teaching the dancing on this dance show, he had been in front of the cameras for years and so it felt like he was guiding me. He still had to learn how to dance, however, and he did – he just took his own time. I was very patient with him and I would never, ever criticise him or raise my voice and he tried to learn as much as possible.

Soon I started noticed changes in him, too, like his eating habits. When we first had lunch together, he would have lots of bread with his meal and a glass of wine, but then he started to drop some of the bread and I encouraged him to drop the wine, too. He started losing weight (he had lost 30 pounds by the end of the show) and he felt a lot better in himself; it also helped him not to get out of breath so much. We were spending a lot of time rehearsing, about seven or eight hours in training a day, as it did take time for him to learn a routine – I don't think he had ever done that much physical activity in his life!

With John I choreographed every single thing and I had to be quite clever with the routines I put together. I purposely played on the fun aspects of the dances, and in our third dance, the samba, I chose the music, 'Papa Loves Mambo'. As it was such fun music we put a lot of playful moves into it. One of those moves was for John to dance a little bit on his own – only for sixteen beats of the music, but totally on his own – and he didn't have a clue what to do so he ended up flinging his arms above his head. It was hilarious!

That was the best thing about John – he was up for anything and he trusted me completely. He wasn't afraid to do what I asked him to do, even if that meant he would look silly. And I think that was what made him so endearing to the public: they realised he was never going to be a good dancer but he was an incredible entertainer. And he was the one who taught me, on my very first series, the real purpose of the show: entertainment. That is something that a lot of dancers and most of the celebrities who take part don't understand: it is purely an entertainment show. For me the penny dropped after a few weeks, as before then I was still in the competitive dancing frame of mind. I was coming from a world where the dance had to be of the highest quality, where the technique had to be spot-on and the precision immaculate. But John was the one who 'got' the show – this wasn't a world-class dancing competition, it was an entertainment show for television.

I knew that it was my job to make funny, great routines, as there was no one else like John in the cast that year – there were lots of good dancers but there was no one who could be funny like him. All our routines were fun and none more so than our now infamous paso doble. I think from that moment on, the show changed in its viewpoint; people had been watching it before to see the dancing; now they were watching it and seeing that dancing was fun. And John and I were definitely having fun!

CHAPTER 16

Dancing with John is a drag (paso doble week)!

There is always a lot of hype over couples breaking up and others coming together on *Strictly Come Dancing*. It is the closeness, the physicality of dancing with someone of the opposite sex that gets people talking. And I understand that if you are new to dancing, new to this whole concept of putting yourself in someone else's arms, it can be perceived as something sexual. But as a professional dancer, having grown up in this business for years, a close proximity to someone else is very normal. We don't feel threatened or intimidated by it or take it as a sexual tension of any kind. That personal space line that people have is so blurred for all of us dancers because we grow up dancing so close to other people. We feel each other's bodies and we are trained to understand body signals… It's a non-verbal communication and as professionals, something we have been developing for years and years.

When I first started dancing on *Strictly*, I didn't think twice about it. Why would the physical closeness be perceived as strange? Why would other people find it so difficult? And with John, we had quite a father-daughter relationship so I never thought about it. The press started joking about how wonderful it must be for John, an old man, dancing with this young blonde girl and I just thought, 'What a silly thing to say!'

He was a sixty-four-year-old man whom I saw as a father more than anything else. But I guess I was a little naïve and he was very comfortable with it – besides, all of our dances weren't based on any intimacy, only comedy. I did think a couple of the costumes I was given to wear were a little skimpy and it felt a little inappropriate to wear them to dance with John so I made sure they didn't give me any two-piece dresses to wear – I was always covered a little more.

I understood very quickly that John was very well liked and had his own fan base. I wanted to appeal to them too, and I didn't want him to lose that support. He introduced me to a lot of his friends who were journalists and in my eyes everyone was a friend, even members of the press.

All the experiences with the media I had at that point with John were positive and we were progressing through the show, too. We got through the second week, the third week, the fourth week… I thought to myself, 'This is just insane!' Of course I wanted to stay in for as long as possible but to me it was surreal as there were such good dancers on the show and we were doing entertaining and clever comedy sketches, really. But it wasn't like we weren't working hard: John was learning a lot and his ability definitely improved. So I said to myself, I just need to make my

routines interesting, make a good impression as a professional –
this job is only for four months so just enjoy it! I didn't want to
be famous; I was going back to LA in December so I always had
that in the back of my mind.

And then things started to go wrong. I began picking up a
few bad vibes from the other professional dancers and I knew
they were annoyed by the fact we were still in the show even
though John wasn't very good at dancing. There were decent
dancers leaving the show and it became a little uncomfortable.
And then the press started picking up on the same idea: that
this old man who couldn't dance was staying in a dancing show
while other, better dancers were leaving. They began calling
him 'the dancing pig in Cuban heels' in the stories they were
writing about him. To me, this was just rude.

The judges weren't giving us any positive comments either,
not that I ever expected they would. They were quite harsh
but it was the rudeness I couldn't understand. There was John,
a well-respected gentleman and let's be honest, some of the
judges were of a similar age, so I thought the rude comments
were just inappropriate. But then again, I was new to the show
and I didn't appreciate how it worked on TV – that someone
had to be a villain, for example. In the competitive world, you
don't ever get a comment from the judges, you just receive your
scores after your dance and even then it is what we call 'closed
judging' whereby you don't know who gave you what scores. It
was all very different from TV judging.

I knew Len Goodman from *Dancing with the Stars* and on
TV in America but I didn't know Arlene Phillips, Bruno Tonioli
or Craig Revel Horwood. It was funny, though: the harsher the
judges were to John, the more the public showed their support

for him. It was the public versus the *Strictly* judges. And John wouldn't ever let me say anything back to the judges. He always managed to make light of it and whenever we were interviewed by *Strictly*'s co-presenter Tess Daly afterwards he made a few jokes about what they had said. I am sure that is why he was so well liked with the public because they could see that he wasn't taking any of the judges' comments too seriously – he didn't have anything to prove.

The further we got into the competition, though, the more uncomfortable it became. John told me that the paparazzi would be camped outside their house trying to take pictures of his wife and two sons. Mary, his wife, was lovely and she never wanted that sort of attention. If you are not in the world of television it is not something you are used to or ask for and I knew she was constantly being asked by reporters, 'What do you think of your husband dancing with a young Russian blonde?' or 'What do you think about him being in the competition for so long? He is so rubbish!'

I couldn't believe it when John told me all of this. Who would benefit from all those negative stories? I couldn't understand why, when you had this brilliant show on TV that everyone loves, it was so important for the press to write something negative and so rude, too. And why would they want to make fun of someone like John?

Around that time I was asked to do an interview with the *Daily Mirror*. It was a solo interview just about beauty tips and make-up and I have always been into health and beauty and new products so it was really exciting for me. I did it with the BBC press office sitting in on the interview and then waited for it to appear in the Sunday supplement magazine. I couldn't quite believe it when I read the article, it made me sound so cheap and tarty. It was written in a very sarcastic way and used quotes that I never actually said! My character had never been judged before: it was always about my dancing, or my choreography or teaching. I asked John about it and he just explained that the press can be on your side one minute and then the next, completely crush you. He told me to embrace it while I was on the show but if I ever found it too hard, just quit.

When I was teaching back in LA, I made sure everyone had a good experience with me as we got pupils through word-of-mouth. If you are difficult to work with then you are unlikely to get new students and I was always very conscious of this. But now I was slowly beginning to understand how the press worked. I was very upset for John too and I was beginning to see a little bit of sadness in him. We were about halfway through the competition and although he was still trying his hardest to learn, he wasn't having as much fun in rehearsals: his heart simply wasn't in it.

After getting through the samba in Week 5, I then got the news from the producers that we would be dancing the paso doble in Week 6. The paso doble! I didn't have a clue how it would work, since the whole dance revolves around the male character, who has to be a strong bullfighter type and very aggressive in his moves and facial expressions. How could I do this with John? So I decided to keep the music fairly traditional and go back to basics. I used a technique called 'bronze level figures' whereby I would teach him just a few steps and he had to repeat them over and over again. Then I thought it would be good to include something exciting at the beginning of the routine, a talking point. With my previous partners we had done a move where I drop to the floor and my dance partner swoops me around on the floor and then picks me up again. Obviously it was quite fast and looks exciting when two professionals are dancing it, but John couldn't even pull me.

We did a few rehearsals with this move and decided to keep it in the routine and then my plan was to do a lot of dancing around him. At least the 'drag' would take up a bit of time in the music and then he could concentrate on the basic steps I taught him. When we came to the dress rehearsal on the Friday at the BBC Studios, I could hear people giggling around us. I couldn't work out what was so funny until they said that as he wasn't even able to pull me, it just looked like I was lying on the floor while he was kicking me in the forehead. So I said to him he really needed to try and pull me as far as he could so I wouldn't just sit on the same spot on the dance floor.

Well, when we actually performed on the night the whole studio went mad! Some were laughing, some were clapping, but I think everyone appreciated John having a go at this iconic dance. Here was a man who couldn't really pull me across the floor and instead of looking aggressive he just managed to look grumpy. When I watched the show back later, I understood why there was a standing ovation afterwards. It was just so funny and he only managed to pull me a couple of steps, bless him! But he gave it a good go and that is what the show is about.

I have learnt now, after all my years on the show, that working with a celebrity partner is all about trust. This is my world the celebrity is coming into, my knowledge I am teaching, my choreography, my skills they have to learn. And in the past I have had celebrities who don't want to let go and they take themselves quite seriously and it never works.

John made people realise that *Strictly* isn't just for the young, fit, good-looking types, anyone can enjoy it. I had so many fan letters from viewers who wrote to us saying things like, 'I've just booked some dance lessons for my dad who is retired and he's really enjoying it'. Older couples wrote to us saying how much we had inspired them to take part and start dancing together and there was a lady from Scotland who wrote to us, telling us she had just bought two kittens and one was really big and one was really small so she had named them John and Kristina!

People were genuinely interested in what we were going to do next and John always said to me that the British public are very smart and clever and they will not support anyone that they don't think deserves it. He said that he would keep doing the show all the time the public still wanted him to.

But after the Paso Doble Week, even though we might have had the public on our side, the press started to turn. We were facing a bit of a backlash: 'Why is the Dancing Pig still in the show?' was the general consensus. I was getting lots of press attention and I felt quite unnerved by it all and the BBC didn't want me talking to anyone.

And so we kept going. Bruce Forsyth was always very nice to John and me and he opened the show one week with the words, 'Welcome to the John and Kristina Show!' which I don't think the producers liked but it was nice to think he was on our side.

We danced the foxtrot in Week 7, Week 8 was the cha-cha-cha and Week 9 was the American smooth. This dance required a lift, a little cradle lift in a baby-doll position, and I remember

Craig Revel Horwood commenting that John wasn't that bad! Craig said he could actually see some improvement. It tends to happen like that: Week 5 and Week 6 are a pivotal point for the celebrities because if they can make it that far then they tend to feel a lot less nervous about being on the dance floor and start to embrace it.

Unfortunately, while we were still being kept in the show by the public there were a number of dancers who were getting better scores than us who were being voted off and that made me feel really uncomfortable. I do know that some of the professional dancers were saying nasty things behind my back and that the celebrities became very open about how they felt about John and me still being on the show.

I did get quite defensive as I didn't understand how this was our fault – I was just doing a job with John and if people wanted to keep on voting for us then who was I to stop it? It was very intimidating, though, and because I was the new girl on the show, I was still desperate to fit in. Apart from Brian I didn't have any proper friends there and he was busy focusing on his dance partner, singer Heather Small, so we didn't really get to see each other.

I did feel like an outcast at several points. The only person I could talk to was my mum but it was hard to explain to her what was going on in this British TV show. It was in such a different world so it was very hard to understand.

John was definitely not enjoying it any more. He started saying to me, 'The fun is over, it's all becoming a little bit too aggressive and not nice for the both of us.'

We got to the week before the quarter-finals and our next dance was the salsa. I started putting a routine together and one afternoon, I sensed a real change in the atmosphere. There was no laughing or joking and when we took a break, John told me he was finding it difficult and struggling to see the fun side – especially as the media had started hounding his family. I remember being followed home by a paparazzo on a motorbike one evening and it was quite petrifying. As soon as I got home I had to call my mum – I couldn't believe quite why I was interesting enough for him to be following me. Of course it meant that the paps all knew where I lived and so I started finding more and more of them outside the flat waiting for me.

The day after one of our early rehearsals for the salsa I left John with a feeling in my gut. I went to bed with that feeling and I couldn't shake it off. We had arranged to meet the following morning bright and early for rehearsals but when I woke up at 7am, I already had a text message from him waiting for me.

It said: 'Kristina, I have been up all night. I'm really, really sorry but I feel like the right decision would be for me to step down and finish the show. The joke has gone a little bit too far. But before I say any of that to anybody I need to know that you are OK with this decision as I don't want to hurt you and I don't want to hurt your career and it is very important to me that you are OK with this decision.'

The funny thing was I wasn't surprised. I knew something like this was brewing so I texted him back straight away: 'John, I completely understand. I will support you no matter what. We are a team and we've been a good team and I don't want you to be unhappy. We have created great numbers that will live in *Strictly* history and so I completely support you and I will be there for you.'

I was touched that he was concerned about my feelings but

there was a part of me that thought this was as good a time as any to stop. It was nearly the quarter-finals and if we did make it through, we would have to learn two dances a week. That would be extremely hard because we could barely do one dance a week and it wouldn't be fun any more if he was feeling like this; he wouldn't be happy. The press had completely blamed him the past Saturday night for the public voting-off of the English actress Cherie Lunghi and her partner James Jordan, who were good dancers. No one seemed happy that we were still in the competition and I understood that John was bearing the brunt of the backlash. He told me he was going to call the producers and arrange a press conference that day.

'The craziest thing is, Kristina, I don't want to win the show, I don't want to be in the final,' he told me.

I am sure I had seen that the bookmakers had shortened the odds that we might win the show and for John that very real possibility was quite scary. 'The joke has gone too far,' he said. 'I understand that the public want to prove they have the power over the judges on voting but enough is enough.'

After I had received those text messages and John had spoken to the BBC about the press conference I remember turning on the BBC News and I could not believe what I was seeing. There was video footage of John dragging me across the floor in our paso doble routine being shown with the caption, 'Breaking News: John Sergeant quits *Strictly Come Dancing*'. Every fifteen minutes or so it was being broadcast and I couldn't believe it – it was like the Prime Minister had resigned or something.

It was crazy to see myself under that 'Breaking News' slogan and I just couldn't understand why people thought it was such a big deal that John had left the show. But I suppose it just showed how much of a big deal it was – there were millions of people voting for him and he needed to explain his decision.

The press conference was quite surreal. There were probably about thirty journalists there, including Jeremy Paxman, an old friend of John's, asking lots of questions. But John's statement was very concise:

> *If the joke wears thin, if in fact people take it very seriously and if people really are getting so wound up that it's very difficult to carry off the joke then I think it's time to go. It's when you decide when you leave a party, and the time to leave a party is before the fight starts. I think that's what happened on this occasion.*

I had been instructed not to talk to the press by the BBC so I was just sitting there but it was important to me that I was there so it didn't look like John was doing this all by himself. And I didn't want people to speculate that I was angry about it. One journalist did ask me what I felt about it. I said that I supported John and I knew it was the right decision for him to make. There were lots of articles written after his press conference that were pretty horrible – 'Selfish John lets Kristina down' was the main vibe. But they had got it all wrong. If anything, John helped me to have a really good experience on my very first show. It was challenging to choreograph dance routines for a sixty-four-year-old journalist who couldn't dance and I felt like I had done a really good job with him.

It was agreed that we would dance our goodbye dance that following Saturday and so we danced the waltz from Week 1 again. I do remember crying afterwards. It was very sad and we were such a good team and I had had such a lovely time with him. And yes, I did feel like he was a father figure to me and he really took me under his wing.

And do you know what the funniest thing is? If we had ever been in the bottom two then the judges would have booted us off and that would have been that. But we never were in a dance-off, not once – the public saved us every time.

I suppose to some extent I blamed the press: they were all with us at the beginning and then they turned against us and I felt angry because I didn't see why they had to make this man feel so embarrassed about dancing with me on a Saturday night. And they weren't satisfied with his reasons for quitting the show either. They wanted to write stories that speculated 'the real reason John quit *Strictly*!'

I wasn't talking to the press as I wasn't allowed to do so and John made it clear he wouldn't be doing any more interviews after his press conference, so where else did the press turn to get a story? My family. I suddenly started getting phone calls from the press, telling me that they had spoken to my ex-boyfriend, or they had spoken to my dad or they had spoken to an old friend… it was horrific. All of a sudden they were trying to get a quote from anyone I knew. I felt completely cornered as I was forbidden to talk to them by the BBC and yet on the other hand I had the phone ringing off the hook every ten minutes asking me to talk (and I still don't know how they got my number). I started not answering the telephone and then I would get messages that became quite aggressive. They would say things like, 'We have this angle on you from your old boyfriend and if you don't talk to us, we will print this or we will print that about you.'

Where had all this come from? It felt completely horrendous – I was sitting all alone in my flat, crying my eyes out and I couldn't understand why this was happening to me. I didn't want to be threatened, I didn't want my private life all over the papers – for goodness' sake, who would care about that? It was such a horrible, horrible feeling.

So I spoke to John as I just didn't know what to do. He told me to try and ignore it and that it would eventually blow over but it might be a bit rocky for the next few weeks. But then when I saw an article in a newspaper with a quote in it from my dad I was beyond hurt. I didn't even speak to him that often – we had tried to patch things up when I was in America and yes, I suppose you could say we now had an amicable relationship but I was never talking to him on a daily basis. He had called my mum to ask what was happening with me and she had told him that I was really upset as my partner had had to stop doing the show for several reasons and how sad I was because of all the press attention I was getting. That is all my dad knew: he only ever knew what my mum had just told him, I never talked directly to him.

It was so hurtful to see that my father had spoken to the press. When I rang him, he told me that he didn't mean any harm by it and that the journalists had spoken to him and told him how much they adored me; how well I had done in teaching one of Britain's national treasures to dance. And so naturally my dad (who is of course still proud of me and what I have done) said, 'Yes, she is unhappy about not dancing any more.' They made up the rest of the quote from him and used it in the story.

I know how desperate they must have been to get a story,

but I just couldn't understand it. When the *News Of The World* called me I actually told them, 'This is what happened: John was an extremely nice person to work with, I knew he wasn't happy any more', and I told them about the text I got and how I was supportive of his decision. So that is what I said. Then on the Sunday I read something entirely different: 'Exclusive!' it said, 'Kristina opens up about John quitting *Strictly*!'

And I was so naïve: I had tried to give them what they wanted, by simply telling them what had happened and then all of a sudden it was a big 'exclusive'. And it all became so very twisted. It was a rude awakening to the power of the press and I didn't like the fact they went to my family, too: they had tried to speak to my mum, my grandfather (who by this time was well into his seventies) and my aunt, who told me she had had a phone call from a newspaper saying they wanted to find out what sort of child I was. How was that relevant? I just don't understand why there isn't some kind of law that forbids all of that, why they can get away with it.

It was at that point when I had had enough. 'That's it,' I thought. 'I'm not going back to the show if they ask me to return next year. I don't want to go through this again and I don't want to put my family through anything like this again.' All the couples returned for the final show and I did a little dance with John, which was nice but didn't feel as happy as it should have done.

At Christmas I went back to LA and had a good think about my experience overall on the show. I said to my mum, 'I don't think I want to go back. It was hard dealing with the press and I don't think I could deal with it again.' Besides, they might not want me back on the show either!

Being back in LA and with my mum was just what I needed. I met with a few of the producers who were working on *Dancing with the Stars* and they asked me to do a screen test for that show. Mum was really encouraging and wanted me to give it my best shot so I did. It was the same interview that I had done with *Strictly* really – I had to talk about my choreography, how I would teach, my time on *Strictly* and all that. And they told me they would be in touch.

I had high hopes about something positive coming out of that as *Dancing with the Stars* was based in LA so I could live with my mum and I felt it would be amazing.

In January 2009 I was invited to do the *Strictly Come Dancing* tour. I wasn't going to have a celebrity dance partner but I would be doing the group numbers and also solo numbers with a professional dancer, Matthew Cutler. Brian wasn't asked to do the tour so I danced with Matthew, who had previously won the show with singer Alesha Dixon in 2007. It was six weeks on the road and so I went back to England to do it, thinking if nothing else it was a good income for a short period of time and it was exciting to dance on my own, too. All the other dancers had known each other for years but I was still the new girl, desperate to prove that I belonged.

During the tour I did hear back from *Dancing with the Stars*, which was all very positive, and they wanted me to sign a contract that basically said they wanted me on board but there would be no guarantees that I would be used on the show. It was a five-year contract and it meant I couldn't do any other TV work – even though there were no guarantees that I would be on the show. I would be 'on the books' as it were. But I just didn't want to be contracted to *DWTS* for five years with no guarantees so I decided to turn it down. I then made the decision to call the producers of *Strictly* and be totally honest and ask whether they thought they might want to use me for anything in the future. And they were really understanding and said that yes, they were interested in using me – either just for the tours or possibly on the show or maybe in another guise. So I thought, 'OK, I definitely won't sign the *DWTS* contract and when this tour is over, I'll go back to LA, spend a bit of time with Mum and see what *Strictly* then offers.'

Of course, there was the small matter of the tour to get through, which wasn't a problem now as by that time the press had given up on any John Sergeant stories and I was being left well alone. That is, until a professional dancer the press liked to dub 'the Italian Stallion' started getting friendly…

CHAPTER 17

The biggest mistake

The 2009 tour was hard. I was still the new girl and I was still trying to find my place on a show that was well established. Obviously I had been through the mill in the media too with the whole John Sergeant episode, and I remember just feeling so desperate to fit in on the tour: I wanted to be part of the group.

They were all nice and welcoming but most of them were in couples so to speak, either married or with partners, and the only two single people drifting around were Vincent Simone and me. He was very friendly and invited me to lunch several times as he seemed to want company. Whenever we went out to eat, though, all he talked about was how heartbroken he was over his ex-girlfriend Flavia Cacace, who had split up with him for her celebrity dance partner, the *EastEnders* actor Matt Di Angelo. At that stage, he just needed a friend to talk to, someone to open up to, and I was happy to listen to him. He seemed very broken inside and needed a friend. And I was craving someone's consideration too, just to feel I wasn't alone.

Yes, it was a mistake but he was very charming and he was paying me a lot of attention. I wanted someone to share my stories with and to talk to. Those desperate feelings of wanting to belong overshadowed any sort of common sense that I might have had about the situation. In my defence, he acted like a single guy and totally dismissed that he was in any sort of relationship or that he had anyone in his life. He never said he had a girlfriend; he said there was a girl who was very much in love with him and that it was complicated. I couldn't really understand why he kept saying that; I think at the time I thought it was 'complicated' because he still had feelings for Flavia. Of course now I feel it was stupid of me to fall for it all, but I did.

Whenever we would go out as a big group after a show I would spot this girl sitting by herself, never trying to be with Vincent. And he was always at the bar, chatting up other girls. To me that didn't look like a relationship – in my mind he was acting like a single man and I didn't have any reason not to trust him. I was very vulnerable at that time and when you are on tour with the same people, day in and day out, it's a surreal world. It makes you think you are very close to people and I did feel like I was bonding with Vincent. I didn't think anyone could lie so blatantly, or maybe he did believe the things he said, I don't know. Anyway, he gave me a couple of gifts and gave me the attention I was craving so it wasn't hard for me to give in to it. But it was just the most ridiculous thing to do and I feel so very embarrassed by it.

Family and friends are so important to me and I try to visit them as often as I can. *Above*: Here I am with my aunt's children, Andrey and Ksenia in Russia.

Below: My best friend Alex and her son Maxim, who is my godchild. Alex lives in Seattle and I met her when she came to me for dance lessons.

Above: I loved working with John Sergeant. He was the only celebrity I have worked with who never seemed nervous – he just wanted to have fun!

Below left: The infamous drag in our paso doble, which had the *Strictly* audience whooping and cheering.

Below right: I won my first *Strictly* trophy dancing the quickstep with John Barrowman in the Christmas special in 2010.

© *BBC*

Above left: Backstage with Jason Donovan, with whom I made it to the final in 2011.

Above right: Performing the Viennese waltz with Colin Salmon in Week 2, 2012.

Below left: Waltzing with Ben Cohen, my partner in *Strictly* 2013.

Below right: Backstage with Simon Webbe in our costumes for the Charleston, which we performed in the final in 2014.

Above left: Posing with Ola Jordan and Anya Garnis.

Above right: Backstage with other professional dancers (*left to right*) Artem Chigvintsev, Pasha Kovalev, Katya Virshilas and my partner Robin Windsor after a group performance.

Below: Rehearsing with Robin during a trip to South Africa in 2015, where we represented BBC Worldwide at corporate events.

Above: Jazz hands! Rehearsing for
Burn the Floor, which ran at the
Shaftesbury Theatre in 2013.

Middle: Performing a dramatic routine
during a photocall for the show.

Right: Robin and I at the after party,
held at the Trafalgar Hotel, following
the press night performance on
11 March 2013. *© Getty Images*

My work with Dot Com Children's Foundation means the world to me, and in 2014 I decided to hold a fundraising event in London.

Left: Inside Mansion House with (*left to right*) Anton Du Beke, Iveta Lukosiute, Judy Murray, Aljaz Scorjanec, Janette Manrara, Thom Evans and Karen Hauer. I had to give a speech straight after Cherie Blair – not daunting at all!

Right: Robin and I with charity founders Sharon and Neil Evans, Kathryn Blair and Tony Blair.

Courtesy of Dot Com Children's Foundation

Left: Sharon and I with her *Best* magazine Bravest Women Award.

Above: With my best friends Alex and Irina.

Below: Me and my mum, Larisa, the strongest woman I know. © *Best Magazine*

Above: Simon and I were ecstatic to become champions of *Strictly's* live arena tour in 2015, winning the Glitterball trophy.

© *Matrix Pictures*

Below: In many ways, I feel I owe my existence to dancing. The dance floor is my home and where I feel most comfortable.

On the last day of the tour he asked me to come into his room. I was due to fly back to LA the very next day to see my mum and I thought we were going to talk about what would happen with the relationship now the tour was ending, but I could not have been more wrong. He simply said: 'The girl that I told you about, she is my girlfriend and I can't leave her now because she is pregnant.'

I felt absolutely sick to my stomach; my legs almost gave way, they were shaking so much. At first I thought someone was playing a cruel joke on me – this could not be happening, it must be untrue. I asked him if he had just found out about her pregnancy and he was honest enough to say 'no' and that she was 'four months pregnant'.

I can't describe how I felt – I just knew how revolting the whole situation was.

I vaguely remember him then saying to me that he was still going to try and finish with her but it is a bit of a blur, to be honest, and I don't remember what I said to him.

I was so upset, so angry and sad, and I just felt completely used. It was a real mess and I didn't think anything like that would ever happen to me but in a sense at least it was between us and I could fly back to LA and get away from it all. But that wasn't to be the end of it: his girlfriend took her story to the press and the whole situation became much, much worse. I went back to LA and started receiving some very angry messages from them both. I'm ashamed to say I sent back a lot of angry ones, too – more in a defensive way, but that is no excuse.

If Vincent had been any sort of man about this, he would have stood up and taken responsibility for the whole mess. All he had to do was say, 'Yes, this is my fault.' But he never did

173

and the whole situation got so aggravated when she took her story to the press.

It was disgusting, it was very hard to read, and I was in the States seeing it all on the internet. I remember reading that they had separated for a while and she left him – I didn't blame her. I was so angry with him but I think I was angrier with myself for trusting someone so easily. I was fooling myself thinking that he really cared because he was always taking me out to lunch and dinner and giving me presents and paying me a lot of attention. If I could go back in time and change it, I would. I cannot explain how disgusted I felt with myself.

If I'm honest, I did think that maybe I should just forget *Strictly* altogether and stay in America but at the same time I was scared not to have a steady job as I still felt the responsibility of supporting my family, the desire to help my mum. Working was still a driving force in me and my aunt persuaded me to accept the job. The producer told me they didn't care about all the media attention I had been getting. She said she knew what the press was like but the important thing was that they wanted me on the next series. 'We know you are an amazing dancer and we want you back on the show,' she reassured me. 'You have to think about the job you are doing. The press is the press, it will always be there and you won't be able to do anything about it but you just have to move forward. We want you back as we think you're really good as a performer and a choreographer and we don't want to see you waste your talent.'

And that made me feel better. I was also offered a massive pay-deal to tell my side of the story to the *News of the World*.

I was supposed to show all the text messages and emails from Vincent's girlfriend and Vincent that they had sent me. In them

I was verbally abused and called lots of horrible names and yes, I reacted badly and I was saying horrible things back, which was so stupid. But I had had enough and I thought, 'You know what? I want to tell my side of the story.' I was offered a lot of money and this was my chance to say everything I needed to say. So it was all arranged and the morning of the interview I woke up, went into the bathroom and looked at myself in the mirror… and that is when I realised, I just couldn't do it. What good would ever come of it? I would just be in the same category as all the people who go to the press and sell their kiss-and-tell stories and I would degrade myself even more. And then I would be at a point of no return. If I sold my story and put all those text messages out for the public to see, what good would it do? And I would always have the feeling that I sold a bit of myself to a tabloid newspaper.

So I decided not to do it and it did not go down at all well with the newspaper. I was harassed and they tried to persuade me to still do the story by bullying me to a certain degree. They told me that if I didn't tell the story they would write other things about me but that was a risk I was willing to take. I didn't want to sell this story any more and I was prepared for whatever they were going to do. Sure enough, they did pay me back a few years later.

It is funny how life works, though. The same day I turned down the newspaper deal and spent all morning and afternoon crying and feeling sorry for myself, I got a phone call from Brian Fortuna in the evening. He told me he had just started working on a new BBC3 show, *Dancing on Wheels*, which was a one-off six-episode series about ballroom dancing for wheelchair users commissioned for Disability Month. 'Kris, I really need your help. It's going to be a lot of work and I really need help in teaching these guys,' he said. Brian had quite a lot of knowledge of wheelchair dancing as his parents had set up a dance school in LA for wheelchair-users. I was quite flattered that he asked me to help him.

At first I said no, I felt like I was in such a bad place. I didn't feel like going somewhere and being filmed and I didn't think I would be any help either.

'Kris, just do one day! Come and do one day with me and if you don't like it, don't sign the contract,' said Brian.

So I did and I went to Brunel University, where the whole thing was being filmed. When I walked in I saw a young guy in a wheelchair, who was paralysed from the waist down. His name was Harry and he was twenty-four years old and he was such a nice guy. He was waiting to meet his celebrity and I just choked. I just looked at him and it seemed so unfair for someone so young and sweet to be sitting there in a wheelchair. I turned to Brian and just said, 'I'm really sorry but I just don't think I can do it, I just don't think I am strong enough to do it.'

And he said to me, 'Kris, these people don't need your pity, they just need your help with dancing. They are so excited and you can help them with that, you can be part of this experience with them. Don't you want to be that person?'

And well, how could I say no? In fact I fell in love with the project – I was so involved with everyone we worked with and they were all such amazing people. It was six weeks of filming and rehearsing throughout June and the first two weeks of July in 2009 and I got paid hardly anything for it but the experience and the people… They gave me something more than an income: in a sense they put me back together again and very quickly I realised that I had no problems in my life, I had nothing to be upset about at all. For me it put such a massive perspective on things as at the end of the day, I can get up in the morning and walk and dance and do what I love for a living.

I loved that project, it was a very special experience and I was so pleased to be part of it. It was a blessing in disguise and I was very proud watching them all perform. And funnily enough, the winner of the series was a certain Caroline Flack! I worked with her and trained her throughout the show and she won the series with her partner James, who was a double amputee. Of course, it wasn't going to be her last victory on a dancing show…

After the series finished, I thought to myself, 'OK, we all mess up, we all make mistakes. I need to stop feeling sorry for myself now and just get on with things – there is so much more to life. At the end of the day, I love what I do and it is a job that always makes me happy and can make a world of difference to people I work with, like the guys in the wheelchairs.' I felt useful again and I decided that my passion and my talent for dancing were all that mattered.

The show had been a healing process but I felt I needed to have closure on the whole situation with Vincent. And when I say closure, I felt that I wasn't ever going to be able to put it behind me properly until I had spoken to his girlfriend and apologised. Vincent had played us both: we were both lied to and we were both really upset at the time and there was a lot of anger, too. I didn't need to have anything to do with him any more but I knew in my heart that I wanted to apologise to her. It took a few years for me to feel brave enough to pick up the phone but I wanted to say sorry to her, in a sense I felt I needed to explain myself and it was such an important conversation for me to have. I knew her life had been made miserable as mine was miserable too, but I wanted her to know that I was embarrassed and ashamed about the whole situation. It was really good to speak to her and when that conversation took place I was so relieved. I cried a lot and she understood that I was speaking from my heart. She was very gracious and it meant a lot to me that we were able to talk and to have that closure.

I will never forgive Vincent for what he did to me and what damage he did to my reputation. I know he did try a couple of times to speak to me through Robin Windsor, who went on to become my partner. He would tell Robin that he was sad that we couldn't even say hello to each other. But we don't, and I will never forgive him.

CHAPTER 18

A Welsh dragon and a Siberian siren

In the last two weeks of July 2009 I went back to LA to spend time with my mum before the next series of *Strictly* training began. She was happy that I had taken the job again but she did say that I really needed to decide where I wanted to settle – living in between two countries wasn't really ideal!

So as *Strictly Come Dancing* could now lead on to other things, I decided I needed to have my base in London and close the door on my life in America. Mum was going back to her flat and my aunt in Russia and I felt that there would be more opportunities for me in the UK. By then I had rented a one-bed apartment in Bayswater for a year and was ready to get my teeth into a new series, into a new project. The day before I was due to fly back to London, I had convinced myself that the producers were going to give me a celebrity who was so completely under the radar that I couldn't be the subject of any more press or sensational stories and instead, I could just focus on teaching and dancing.

I got a text from one of the producers, who told me that the morning after I arrived, I would have to meet the film crew at the BBC Studios and that I would then be taken to a place called Wales. I had never been to Wales and to be honest, I didn't really know where it was or anything!

So I called my agent: 'The BBC are sending me to Wales! Do you know why? Do you know who I am going to be partnered with?'

He said that there was a list of celebrities that the newspapers were speculating were going to take part and so far the only person who might have the Welsh connection was a boxer called Joe Calzaghe. He had just retired from boxing and so the papers were speculating that he was a possibility for the new series of the show. And my heart just sank. I had a good friend who appeared on *Dancing with the Stars*, who was partnered with a boxer, Floyd Mayweather, Jr. She had told me that they had a very difficult relationship, he was hard to work with and their personalities just didn't click at all. I thought to myself, 'This is going to be awful if my celebrity partner is a boxer like him!'

So I googled Joe as I had absolutely no idea about the world of boxing or who he was and what he had achieved. And the more I read, the more I convinced myself that this guy was going to be such a big-headed, full-of-himself person as he seemed to have won just about every title there was in the boxing world. He was the World Champion, he was undefeated, he'd won this and he'd won that… and I just thought, 'This is going to be a nightmare!'

So my journey to Wales with the BBC wasn't exactly filled with a lot of excited anticipation. I was very nervous about meeting Joe and I was told by the film crew that the official 'meeting' was going to be pretty much like last year. I would walk into a room with a camera crew behind me and meet Joe. We arrived in Wales and went to some tiny village, where Joe was waiting to meet me. And when I walked into this hall and went over to him, he couldn't even look me in the eye! He was so, *so* shy. I walked over to him to say hello and he shook my hand and just said, 'Hi, I'm Joe, nice to meet you.'

And it was a bit awkward after that – we just didn't know what to say to each other. The previous year John Sergeant did all the talking and so I expected the same really from Joe – he was the celebrity after all. But he was really shy and I guess I expected someone who was going to be very outgoing. And so I took charge and I said, 'Right, let's start learning some steps of the cha-cha-cha, which is going to be our first dance.' I wanted to make it fun because it was being filmed for a VT slot to be played on the very first show but he was a little uncomfortable with the cameras and people watching him.

He didn't like it at all and even though he was such a superstar in his field, this was so out of his comfort zone that he struggled a bit. We also had to do a couple of interview sessions afterwards and I remember saying to the cameras that I couldn't believe how shy Joe was and that I hoped it wouldn't change as I had heard such arrogant things about boxers!

The next day we had a full day of rehearsing and Joe brought along his whole family – his mum and dad and his two sisters plus a couple of his friends – to the session. They were very supportive and we went for a meal afterwards to talk about the show and spend time together. I found out that his father was also a musician and that was weird – I hadn't met anyone who had a dad similar to mine. We started laughing about how difficult these musical types can be and I must admit, Joe and I just clicked right away. He was much more outgoing with his family around him and we talked about his boxing and how his dad had trained him all his life.

All our dance training was to be done in Wales so I was staying in a hotel and meeting Joe at rehearsals every day. He took instructions very well and he wasn't afraid to work hard and put in the hours and so we really started to enjoy working with each other. But about a week into rehearsals we started noticing the paparazzi taking an interest in us. They would suddenly appear if we had a break in rehearsals and went out to grab a bite for lunch or something and then we'd see them taking pictures of us walking back into rehearsals. I just couldn't understand it. The penny dropped when I read the stories in the newspaper, speculating on what was going on between Joe and me. It was completely ridiculous as for one, we had only just met and two, whenever we went for lunch we had the film crew with us – not an 'intimate lunch' as the papers reported. By that time my understanding of the media was that this sort of story came with the territory of being on the show but Joe had always had quite an uneasy relationship with the press and hated this personal intrusion. He told me that when he was going through his divorce he had been given a really rough ride by the newspapers and was reported in a very negative light. He's not naïve, he knew because of who he was he would be getting attention, but he couldn't understand why such a private matter, like a marriage breaking up, had to be reported in such harsh detail.

I totally understood and I told him that I still found it fascinating that somebody would want to print a story about me – and why would they? I am just a dancer! Even to this day, it is a mystery. Joe understood my feelings exactly and the more we got to know each other, the more we realised how much we had in common. He came from a very poor family, our fathers were both musicians, and we were both driven from a very young age to be at the top of our game. It gave us a real connection.

In one of the weeks of rehearsals, Joe had to go on a trip and so I had a week off. I invited my friend Alex over from America to spend a week with me in Bath. It was the August Bank Holiday weekend and the show was due to start in a couple of weeks so it was nice to have a bit of a relax before rehearsals went crazy. But on the Sunday evening I got a text from Joe saying he was back in Wales and wanted to train. It was a little weird but Alex understood that I had to put work first so I said yes and headed back to Wales. But when I met him Joe was really distraught. He told me that he had split up from his girlfriend quite a few months ago but they were still in touch over text and she wanted to get back with him. When he had met up with her and told her he was taking part in the show, they had got papped and now according to him the papers were speculating that they were back together. Joe's agent had released a statement saying they had split up but to be honest, I really didn't see how this would be much of a problem for me. I didn't really care about his private life or any of the details, all I wanted to do was to work and do my job.

Before the *Strictly* series is launched on TV, all the dancers and celebrities take part in a day of press interviews so that the media can get quotes about how our rehearsals are going and how we feel about our partners. So of course the press asked all about that, as expected, and then I got a lot of questions asking if I was single. So I replied, yes, I was, but I was happy with that as it gave me more time to focus on Joe. Then they asked Joe if he was single, and he said yes, too. And I could just see the journalists think they now had an angle and from that point onwards, every story had us dating. And because the media put us together, the harassment started again and then my mum called to say she had been visited by a guy who had told her that he worked for the *Daily Mirror* in the UK.

'He was such a lovely guy, Kristina,' she told me.

'Of course he was, Mum, but I did say not to talk to them because they can be quite vicious.'

'But he just said he wanted to write a lovely story about you because your birthday is coming up and they think you are doing such a good job on *Strictly*. And apparently all the *Mirror* readers adore you and want to know how I feel about you dating a world-famous boxer.'

'What did you say, Mum?' I asked.

'I said you weren't dating anyone. And he told me that we obviously didn't have a very good mother-daughter relationship if I didn't know that you were dating Joe. So then I told him to leave as I didn't understand his English.'

My mum understands English perfectly. And she was absolutely right: we weren't dating!

The first couple of weeks on the show didn't exactly go brilliantly for Joe. He found the whole experience really uncomfortable – he didn't like the sequins or the tight trousers or the glamour aspect of *Strictly* and he couldn't overcome his shyness when it came to dancing live. It was such a shame as he was so good in training and picked up the routines really well but as soon as he got on the dance floor he just froze. It was like a rabbit in the headlights and I pleaded with him to just try and pretend it was just him and me, back in the training studio in Wales.

He explained to me that he was afraid and how ironic that was. When he boxed in front of 50,000 people in Madison Square Garden, for example, he never felt one jot of fear but he was scared to death to be on that dance floor and to dance with me! It was very sweet to see this huge boxing legend so vulnerable. And to make matters worse, he wasn't getting good comments from the judges either – they kept saying how rigid and awkward he looked on the floor. I just felt really bad for him but I did explain to him several times that he needed to treat the show as a pantomime, that the judges all play a role and they, especially Craig, are more entertaining when they are nasty. I didn't want him to get too upset by it.

The judging panel had its fair amount of press that year, too. Arlene Phillips had left by that point and Alesha Dixon was now on the show. We were all surprised that Arlene had gone but Alesha had such strong credentials, it wasn't really a big deal for the professional dancers. Besides, not everyone on the judging panel had to have a ballroom dancing background. Of course Len Goodman did, but the others were from a performance background only.

Alesha, who had won the show a few years ago, had also trained at an arts school and was a singer and a performer and an amazing hip hop and jazz dancer. To us she had exactly the right credentials but the poor girl got a hideous time in the press and I remember the *News of the World* in particular ripped her to shreds one week, saying some very negative, horrible things about her. I texted her after reading the vile story to show some support: 'I'm so sorry, I know what it is like being on the wrong end of the press but you are doing an amazing job and I hope you are OK. I am here if you ever want to talk,' I wrote.

And she texted me back, thanking me and she told me that I was the only one to text her and that she really appreciated it. I really felt for her because all she did was agree to take on this amazing job – that she was more than qualified for – but the problem was that people were still upset about Arlene leaving. That wasn't Alesha's fault!

Meanwhile Joe and I both wanted to work hard and prove that he was capable of overcoming his fear of the dance floor so we moved our rehearsals to London. He had quite a few commitments in the city and I could stay at my flat so it worked for us both. And yes, as the rehearsals became more intense, we started to relax more and more with each other and it was pretty obvious that we had quite a strong chemistry. I was completely honest with him right from the start and I told him that there was no way I just wanted a fling – I wasn't interested in that at all. If he thought I was the right girl for him, then this had to be more than an affair otherwise we should just remain friends and carry on with the job. He understood that and he told me he respected the fact that I had been honest with him. Apparently he had had women throwing themselves at him a lot during his life and he never had to fight to get attention from them so the fact that I could take him or leave him at that stage was, he said, quite refreshing.

I also told him that it wouldn't do us any good if we started dating while we were still on the show, it just wouldn't work. It didn't stop how we felt about each other, though and on my birthday he bought me a massive bunch of red roses and we went out for the evening with a big group of friends; it was a wonderful night. We were definitely falling for one another and having spent a month together by that time and seen each other vulnerable, stressed and insecure, you do feel quite close to that person.

I think this is why there are so many relationships on the show. It might take you, in normal circumstances in life, a year to get to know someone, but when you are on the show you know that person inside and out within a month because you are with them practically 24/7. Very quickly you see the real person and to see this legend so vulnerable and so insecure, I started feeling very protective towards him. I didn't want him to dwell on what the press was saying or what the judges would say to him and I tried to remind him that he had signed up for an entertainment show. And in the end it didn't really matter as we got voted off the show in Week 5 anyway.

While it was quite sad to be leaving the show, he was single, I was single and we weren't doing any harm to anyone so we decided to start dating properly. It felt like we could breathe a little bit and we could see each other but without the pressure of learning to dance. And then he told me he would love to take me to Rome for a short break so we went for three days as I had to get back to rehearsals for the group dances. When we got back to the UK, we saw pictures of us together outside the Colosseum.

The press attention was becoming more intense and it didn't

help that his ex-girlfriend was selling stories left, right and centre accusing me of stealing her man. The press were quick to report that I was involved in a cat fight with his ex-girlfriend, even though I didn't respond to any of the accusations or speak out publicly at all. I was accused of breaking up this relationship which was really upsetting to read as Joe's agent, Paul Stretford, released an official statement saying that they had split up weeks before the series of *Strictly* started. The official statement read: 'We can confirm that Joe and Jo-Emma split earlier in August. They remain supportive of each other.' Once again the press were happy to spin a story to keep the gossip going.

By now it was the end of October and we were officially dating. I finally felt I had found someone who understood me because we had been brought up in such a similar way. It was a beautiful relationship and Joe was just the kindest person I had ever met. We fell in love with one another quite quickly and we didn't care – we were two young people in love. But we were being followed by the paparazzi and they would chase us in teams so if Joe and I went separate ways, one lot would follow me and then Joe would have another lot following him, too. It was crazy!

That series on the show Brian Fortuna also started dating his dancing partner, *Hollyoaks* actress Ali Bastian, and then the paps started pursuing them, too. There were lots of stories about them in the press and it occurred to me that at no point was anyone interested in writing about the actual dancing on the show.

In November, I went for a medical check, which I tend to do every six months anyway. I felt I had a little pain in the right side of my abdominal area, which didn't seem to be going. To be honest, as a dancer it isn't unusual to have a little pain here, there and everywhere due to what you put your body through but you just carry on with things. Us dancers tend to live with the mantra that if you can still walk, you can still dance! We are all guilty of not listening to or taking care of our bodies but you tend to carry on with things so the pain, which was coming and going, I just put down to a muscular discomfort. The doctor told me she thought everything was OK but as she wanted to be sure she would send me for a scan. And the scan showed that I had a 4cm cyst on my right ovary. I was so devastated – I remember getting back to my flat, seeing Joe and crying and crying.

It was horrific. I just wanted to enjoy my relationship – we were planning our first Christmas together at his house in Wales – and now I had to plan when to have this operation to remove the cyst. I took part in the *Strictly* finals with Joe but straight after the show had finished filming we came home: my surgery was the very next day. It was quite a quick operation and thankfully they discovered that the cyst was benign but I will never forget how scared I was. I was so grateful Joe was around as he drove me back to Wales after the operation and he did everything he could to look after me. I was so thankful to have him in my life, this wonderful, caring and loving man.

Christmas was really special as I spent it with his family, who were very sweet to me. We had such a happy time with his two sisters and mum and dad. Joe really spoilt me, too. He gave me a commitment ring as he said he wanted to show that he was serious about me – he knew that I had been let down by men in the past and this was his way of showing he was serious about me and serious about our relationship.

I was so happy!

In January I had to do the *Strictly* tour and Joe came everywhere with me, which was wonderful. I really wanted him to meet my mum so when the tour finished I took him to meet her and she thought he was lovely. Mum was pleased that I had met someone who was making me so happy and that he was looking after me so well. And she was right – I was happy with Joe and I didn't see that ever changing.

CHAPTER 19

A knock-out blow

Joe and I started living together in London once the 2010 Strictly Tour had finished. He wanted to base himself in the city a bit more as there were quite a few opportunities coming his way so we rented a flat in Notting Hill Gate. That way we could see each other during the week and then at weekends we'd go back to Wales.

Workwise, things were pretty hectic as after the *Strictly* tour in January and February I had my own tour with Brian Fortuna, 'An Evening With Brian and Kristina', around some of the smaller theatres in the UK. And then in April we started a tour called 'Strictly Come Dancing – The Professionals Tour'. Five professional couples from the show toured the UK for eleven weeks – it was insane! Of course, I was happy to have the work but I wanted to spend a lot of time with Joe, too. The contracts for the tours had been signed over a year ago so I couldn't get out of them and to be honest, when I had signed up for them it was nice to have that amount of work lined up. But of course it made it hard to make time for one another as I had all this work going on and he had his sons to see in Wales, too.

So why did he want to move to London with me at the beginning of the year? Well, towards the end of 2009, he had been getting a lot of interest from a group of 'businessmen' who had approached his dad first, saying they were interested in opening up a few clubs with Joe's name as a selling point. They wondered whether he might be interested in any sort of 'Club Calzaghe' partnership and so he went to a few meetings with these guys to find out more. I thought it was a fantastic project and I was very excited for him but every time he had a meeting about the clubs he would come back and say the whole meeting was strange. Apparently they just asked him lots of questions and he wasn't really getting any answers about this new club franchise. He had asked them about a contract but they didn't give him one and again he would tell me he felt uneasy about it all but he wouldn't elaborate.

Then the bombshell dropped. It was Easter weekend at the end of March and Joe got a phone call saying that all the meetings had been set up by the *News of the World* in a tabloid sting. He had been videoed saying he occasionally used cocaine and now the paper was going to run a big story about his drug use. It was a very sad time for Joe – he was extremely upset about letting his family and his sons down and he was mortified by it all. In my time with him there never was a problem with drugs that I ever saw and I told him that I was there for him, as were his whole family. We all stood by him and I tried to reassure him that it would blow over but it was still very upsetting. I loved that man, he was my family and it was ruthless for someone to set up such a hoax in the hopes of getting a story.

Joe had to release a statement saying how sorry he was about letting down all his fans and I know that the *News of the World* then tried to make him a big offer to sell his side of the story but he refused; he just wanted to be left alone. But then his ex-girlfriend sold a story about his cocaine habit at the beginning of April and it just seemed never-ending. I really felt bad for Joe and I didn't want to leave him on his own at that time – he seemed so vulnerable.

In the four years we were together we did only two photo-shoots, both with *Hello!* magazine. We were offered a lot more but I didn't want to do them. By then I was very much classed as 'Joe Calzaghe's girlfriend' in the press, and it always worried me that I was labelled as someone who was with someone else. In my mind we were equals.

Apart from the negative stories that surrounded Joe for the next few weeks, as a couple we were under media scrutiny, too. Because we were both working on different projects, there was a story in the press pretty much every month that we had split up. One month I had dumped him, the next month he had dumped me – it was just ridiculous. During The Professionals Tour, which ran from April until July, we were given a week off at the beginning of June and Joe and I decided to have a few days together in Spain. As I boarded the plane, I got a text from my agent saying that the papers were running a story that Joe had dumped me for another woman. And I thought, 'OK, well, that is quite funny as we are actually boarding a plane together so I am pretty sure we are still together!'

The story was that he was out clubbing with his mates and giving one particular girl lots of attention. When he came out of the club he agreed to have his picture taken with her (and he got that a lot, everyone wanted their picture with him). From that picture the press wrote a story that he had dumped me. In my mind, for once the press would look stupid as we were going on holiday together as a couple so there was no 'dumping', but of course they don't like to admit their mistakes and so when we got to Spain there were lots of paps taking photos of our 'reconciliation holiday'.

From that point onwards I did start thinking to myself, when is it going to end? I knew I had to stop being bothered by those stories as it was bringing me down and it did cause a few arguments between us – it wasn't particularly pleasant reading that we had or we hadn't split up. Anyway, after the holiday we flew back to the UK and I finished the last three weeks of The Professionals Tour. Our last night was in Bournemouth and Joe organised a big night out for the whole cast and crew to celebrate – it just showed how supportive he was of my work and my commitments.

After the tour I had a quick break before it was time to start the new series of *Strictly* and I found out I was being partnered with Goldie, the DJ. Now I don't blame you for not remembering too much about us that series: we were knocked out the very first week! It was quite sad – I didn't think Goldie deserved to be first out, he just needed a bit more time to develop – but I tried to look on the bright side. Us getting knocked out first meant that I did get a chance to spend more time with Joe. And my mum came over to the UK too, so we all had a nice time together. It was also the year Brian Fortuna left the show and I met my new professional dance partner, Robin Windsor. We just clicked straight away and I know he has said in the press that we became best friends very quickly and we did, we love and respect each other a lot. He did tell me though that he was scared of meeting Joe for the first time, too – but they got on fine!

Joe and I had a chance to spend Christmas and New Year together before I started the *Strictly* tour in January, this time partnering Jimi Mistry. He was a fantastic dancer and I was so happy for him and Flavia Cacace when they eventually got married two years later.

The rest of 2011 was a bit of a blur. Again Joe and I juggled seeing each other as Robin and I had various dance commitments across the UK. We did manage a couple of holidays together, but back in the UK, I think the day-to-day life was getting frustrating for him. He was struggling with being papped wherever we went, especially if we were out and about and looking like we were having a good time. The negative cocaine stories were always being dragged up again, too. It was a hard time for him and he was drinking a lot of the time, which I did understand as to a certain extent he was trying to drown his sorrows.

Joe was always like that – he likes to go out, have a few drinks and make sure everyone is having a good time if they are out with him. He is always at the heart of any gathering and unfortunately for me, it did become a little bit of a problem – I am not much of a drinker myself. We did have some fights about his drinking and that was a bit of an eye-opener too, as it highlighted some differences in our personalities. He told me that he had spent twenty-seven years of his life depriving himself of everything – food, drink, fun – because boxing was his priority. He didn't want to live like that any more, he just wanted to have fun, which I understood, but our lives started heading in different directions. I didn't always want to go to nightclubs and drink until 5am and when I did do it, I didn't really enjoy myself.

It's funny how you can be so right for each other in so many ways and yet the timing can be so wrong. Our relationship had blossomed rapidly and we fell in love quickly but Joe had retired a few months before taking part in *Strictly Come Dancing* and all of a sudden he had a lot of free time. He didn't want to work for a while – he wanted to enjoy his newfound freedom – whereas I didn't want to pass up any sort of job opportunities that came my way.

And there was a certain eighties heart-throb who was about to make my working life a lot more intense as the new series of *Strictly Come Dancing* fox-trotted its way back into my life in September of that year…

Series 9 of *Strictly* brought with it some changes to the format and style of the series. There was a new producer on board who transformed it from a very classic dance show into something a lot more showbiz. We could have props, the music could be more interesting and the costumes could be more experimental. All the professional dancers and I were very excited as we thought it would be a lot more like *Dancing with the Stars*, which would make it more appealing to viewers. She also introduced the pairing of the celebrity and the professional dancer as a whole show in itself, which was quite exciting. And no, I know what you are thinking: I swear on my life and my mother's life too, we don't know who we are dancing with until we are paired with them on the show! That is why sometimes we genuinely look so petrified when it's time to be partnered off. We do have to watch our facial expressions actually – there is no chance to be edited if we pull a scared-looking face.

I remember when they announced the celebrities who would be appearing on the show. When I heard Jason Donovan's name I was praying to be partnered with him – I think I just had this weird sixth sense that we would get along. When it was time for the girls to be paired with their male celebrities, the producer came over to the girls who were left and said she wanted us to be a bit more energetic and enthusiastic when it came to meeting our partners. They had paired the male dancers first and she thought it was a bit boring so she said, 'Right, you all look petrified. I need you to do something fun that will boost the audience and make them all cheer and clap like crazy. Kristina, you are good at this sort of thing, the girls will follow your lead. Just go for it and make it fun!'

And I remember thinking, 'Oh my goodness, why me?' So when Bruce Forsyth announced: 'Jason Donovan, stage and screen superstar, eighties icon will be dancing with… Kristina Rihanoff!' I just went crazy. I ran over to him, jumped on him like a mad woman, wrapped my legs around his waist and went totally mental. When I watched the footage back later I was so embarrassed but everyone said to me, 'That is the craziest reaction we have ever seen, but the producers loved it and the audience appreciated it and it just worked.'

And it was a good result for me as I was genuinely excited about dancing with Jason. This was my fourth year on the show and I just wanted to prove what I could do as a choreographer and as a dancer with someone who could potentially be amazing.

Here was someone who had been on the West End stage; he was musical and would have rhythm. I was over the moon and when we had a chance to talk properly, he was very sweet and told me he'd heard I bring out the best in my partners. He promised me that he would work really hard with me. And that was an understatement – he wasn't bothered about the hours we had to rehearse, he would do anything and everything just to be good. I warned him that I was a hard taskmaster too, so we would certainly get along!

Joe was very supportive and he was also pleased that I had a partner like Jason for this series. He knew how much it meant for me to get someone good so I could showcase some of my choreography – he knew that was where I saw my future.

For the next three months the show would take over my life. It was, without doubt, my most challenging year on the series. I soon realised in our first rehearsal that although Jason had a background in musical theatre, he was quite awkward on the dance floor and when I starting teaching him our first dance, the cha-cha-cha, it was clear he wasn't a natural dancer. Yes, he knew how to stand straight with his head up but he didn't have any sort of co-ordination. Unfortunately, the press were on his case before we had even started to rehearse as they were convinced that he had an unfair advantage because he was stage-trained and would be an amazing dancer from the word go. If only!

Coincidentally, it was only after the whole series had been shown that Jason appeared on *Piers Morgan's Life Stories*. I was so glad when they showed an interview with Phillip Schofield, who had worked with Jason in the nineties on *Joseph and the Amazing Technicolor Dreamcoat*.

'Jason Donovan cannot dance!' said Phillip. 'I know because we had the same choreography for *Joseph* and I know this guy could not dance. When I saw him on the first show of *Strictly* my jaw dropped. I could not believe this was the same guy as he cannot dance!'

I was so pleased that it had been made public that while Jason comes from a theatrical background he was never very good at or enjoyed the dancing side of things – it was just too late!

I remember it was the first week of us performing when they asked us to close the show. My heart sank and I knew the expectation was high so I decided I had to come up with the most amazing routine. I started teaching him the cha-cha-cha and he was a little bit awkward at first and knew he wasn't perfect so he insisted we put in a crazy amount of hours. He wasn't scared of hard work! On the Saturday night I was so nervous for him. I always get asked about nerves on the show and my reply is the same: 'Of course I get nervous, but I am not nervous about myself as I know my steps and I know what I can do, but I am nervous for my partner. That is where the fear is as it's a live show and if they forget their steps or forget the routine there isn't much I can do about it.'

And with Jason, I was petrified for him! When they finally announced us, we walked onto the floor to take our places and I squeezed his hand and whispered to him, 'Let's just do it.' He smiled and said, 'Yes, let's do it!' Joe was in the studio audience, which was brilliant and the audience went crazy from the very first step. Jason is a superstar in every sense: he was nervous and shaking but when I watched the footage back, he flashed that million-dollar smile of his and people just went crazy. He danced brilliantly – we received a standing ovation and it was fantastic. And for the first time ever, after three years on the show, my first dance with my partner wasn't criticised by the judges! Even Craig Revel Horwood said something really positive and we got 8s, which was a fantastic score.

I got a text from Jason the next morning saying he wanted to thank me and how Saturday was one of his most memorable nights of his career. And I just replied, 'Jason, this is only Week 1!'

Right from the start of this series I felt like I needed to bring Joe into my world a little bit more. I knew that with all the rehearsing we wouldn't get to see each other very much so it was important to me that Joe and Jason met and felt comfortable with each other. And I asked Jason if his wife Angela could come to our rehearsals too so that I could meet her. She ended up coming every Thursday, like a lucky charm. Sometimes she would bring the children and she was always incredibly supportive: she made me feel that I could go and do my job and be as strict as I needed to be with Jason. Every Saturday night in the audience she would watch and she would come up to me after each show and say, 'Kristina, I don't know how you do it but you make my husband look good! Thank you so much!'

It meant a lot to both of us that Jason's wife and Joe were comfortable with what we were doing as it was going to be a long road ahead of rehearsals and not really spending much time with anyone else. We were top of the leader board in the first, second and third weeks, but then in the fourth week we dropped right down. It was the paso doble and although we weren't bad, we weren't that great either. People started saying maybe Jason had peaked too early and now he was losing it.

The problem was, there were lots of other people on the show who were getting better and I knew he felt a little deflated. But instead of feeling sorry for himself, he wanted to work harder and asked me if we could rehearse for half a day on the Sunday, too. Now Sunday is normally our day off and the dancers use the day to plan and choreograph the next dance so that we are ready to teach our partners on the Monday morning. And as much as I wanted to say no because I wanted to spend time with Joe and get my head around the choreography on the Sunday, I couldn't let Jason down.

If doing a few hours on Sunday morning rather than be stressed on the Monday helped him then I wasn't going to say no. But it meant that from Week 4 onwards, we didn't have one single day off for the duration of the series – it was tough, to say the least. So our new training schedule went something like this: every Saturday night after the show, if we were voted through to the next week, we would receive our music and be told what dance we would be performing next by the production team. We would film the results show on the Saturday night, even though it was not shown on the TV until the Sunday. Sunday would be a day off for the rest of the cast but for Jason and me, we started rehearsing from 10am until 2pm so that on the Monday morning he wasn't so daunted by a new routine.

So when did I get the chance to work out the choreography for this? Basically, after we finished filming on the Saturday night. I would be getting home around midnight and would then work on the choreography until about 3am. After shutting myself in the kitchen so that I didn't disturb Joe, I would put together a new routine ready to teach Jason a few hours later.

201

I was very protective of Jason and I knew how important it was for him to do well on the show. He had been called an 'old, washed-up eighties star' in the press and he really wanted to prove he could do something amazing. To me he was a legend and if I had to be up until the early hours of the Sunday and then work on our only day off, so be it: I wasn't going to let him down. I think that is where my dedication to work and desire to succeed overshadowed my relationship.

Even though Joe was incredibly supportive, we were only seeing each other for a few hours in the evenings and a bit of Sunday afternoons (and I was completely knackered!) so it was challenging. This job comes with a lot of sacrifices and you have to be able to make them or you leave the show. But I was so passionate about the series that there was no question of me not giving it my absolute all.

CHAPTER 20

Too many broken hearts in the world

When you watch just one and a half minutes of a dance on a Saturday night, it's hard to fully comprehend the amount of rehearsing that goes into creating that ninety seconds of performance. And the further you go in the competition, the harder it gets. The training gets more intense, the standard gets higher and if you don't deliver something special each week to capture the audience's vote, you have been through it all for nothing!

I knew how the outcome of this competition would affect Jason. The whole experience on *Strictly* meant a lot to him and he was so driven to succeed. We were very alike in this sense: we would go into the studio and work like crazy, to the extent that even our camera crew started asking us if we wanted to take a break for a minute. They offered to make us cups of tea just so they could see us have five minutes' rest! We were going for it at 100 miles an hour and Jason was so focused on getting everything right there was no time for a pause.

And yes, it did put a lot of strain on my relationship with Joe. I was home but not home – I was there in body but not in spirit. It wasn't a normal relationship, and I accept that I neglected him during the series, but when I have a responsibility to someone professionally that takes priority over everything else; it always has done. Joe was supportive but I know he did feel lonely and left out.

The competition was really full-on that year, too – the standard was very high and sometimes you just felt as if there weren't enough hours in the day to do anything. You might as well not even sleep! When we reached the quarter-finals I remember sensing that every couple was struggling and feeling the pressure. Jason and I, we were barely moving our legs at that point, we were just so exhausted. Quarter-final week was Movie Week and so we did the American smooth to 'Singin' in the Rain'. Everyone seemed to love it but then we found ourselves in the bottom two. You have to be skilled as a choreographer not just to provide the steps but to be able to capture people's attention, too. Jason was such a great showman that I wanted his personality to come across in the routine – it was like in the early days of the show when I had to play on his acting skills before he started developing a proper technique.

The problem with quarter-finals week was that we had also started to put the group Christmas dance together, too. All the couples had to meet on the Monday to rehearse together and Jason was so stressed that we were missing a day of our own rehearsals and he was convinced that he wouldn't be able to learn the routine. He looked like he was on the verge of tears.

I gave him a big hug and tried to reassure him that this was the final stretch, that Angela and his family were behind him and there was so much love and support for him, but he was so stressed, he just didn't feel prepared at all.

That year there was no dance-off, the results were decided solely on the public vote, and we were up against former Wales footballer Robbie Savage and his partner Ola Jordan in the bottom two. I have been in that position many times before (I was expecting to be out every single week with John Sergeant!) and that moment when you are standing there, waiting to learn your fate, doesn't get any easier. The end is in sight, the final is only a week away and you want to be a part of it. But we got through and in a way, reaching the semi-finals was great, but it made us even more stressed. By this point I realised we wouldn't win the show. I think Jason did, too, but we wanted to reach the final, we wanted to continue to put in 110 per cent and see where it got us. We had to dance the samba, notoriously the hardest dance to perform because it is so technically difficult. I thought, 'OK, we can do this. We'll do the samba and the Argentine tango as Jason will be able to play the part well.'

I didn't make the samba too crazy as I wanted to show his fun side and for the viewers to see him happy and enjoying himself. And when we first performed the Argentine tango in the dress rehearsal on the Friday, the producers actually came over to us and said what an amazing routine it was. We had people from the production crew applauding us after the rehearsal and that gave Jason such a boost. They said to him: 'Whatever you do, Jase, you have to go out and dance it in exactly the same way – it was outstanding!'

So when it came to Saturday night, we just wanted to get

the samba out of the way first and dance the Argentine tango! We closed the show with that dance and up until that point, before every performance, I would have to give Jason a bit of reassurance – just a little hug or a few words of encouragement. When we walked out onto the dance floor before the tango, I was about to give him a little pep talk but he just stopped me: 'Kristina, I've got it,' he said. I knew from that point on this dance was going to be amazing. He knew what he was doing and he was ready to perform like there was no tomorrow. The studio went nuts and everyone loved it. Jason was on the verge of tears at the end; it was a magnificent performance. Suddenly the press were saying that Jason did deserve a place in the final. It was the perfect combination of movement and acting and he was brilliant in the role. I was so proud of him and we were eventually rewarded with a place in the final.

Every time I start a new series I am asked by journalists, 'Do you want to win? Do you want to get to the final?' And yes, of course it's nice to say you've won the series, but as a professional dancer, it doesn't really change our lives dramatically. In our dancing world it doesn't really make a difference, but what does make a difference is the impact you make on the show. I would rather have a memorable run with John Sergeant than win the show and be forgotten the following year.

McFly drummer Harry Judd won the show that year with his dance partner Aliona Vilani, and he was brilliant. Handsome and talented, we all knew from the word go he would win as he was so good and everyone adored him. You can't compete with that popularity and Jason wasn't stupid, he knew we wouldn't win but to get to the final, well, that was enough for us.

That year the finals were at the Blackpool Tower. It was the only time they ever did the final there, and while it was brilliant to be dancing in this iconic location, in an already exhausting week it was just an added pressure to travel there and get settled. By then it had been thirteen weeks of rehearsals. When the show starts everyone looks so healthy and raring to go and then by the finals, we're all looking like death because we are so, so tired.

We travelled to Blackpool on the Thursday and then on Friday we had a 7am call to be on BBC1's *Breakfast* via a live link. So we had to be at the Tower and ready at 7am, which means you have to be up and in make-up by 6am. All three couples struggled with this early start! The place is magnificent, though, and there is something so beautiful about it, you do forget the tiredness and the cold – and it was freezing cold that December too, I remember. We had three dances to perform on the Saturday and an extra one to prepare in case we made it through to the final two: our favourite dance, the judges' choice, our show dance and then one you haven't done on the show before. So the fourth dance only happens if you make it to the last two couples, but you still have to prepare one!

When the final started, Joe and his family and Jason's family were there in the audience, and it was really special. Our first dance was the tango to the soundtrack, 'I Will Survive'! All very camp, it was the judges' choice and we loved it. Our show dance got full marks, 10s from all the judges, and it was fantastic. The judges loved it, although I think that Craig thought I was on a mission to kill Jason!

'Jason, you need to charge that woman and lock her up, I can't believe all the things she is making you do,' he told him in a half-joking, half-serious way.

After getting a perfect score from the judges, Jason said to me that maybe there was a chance we would win the show, and it was a bit sad as in my heart I knew this wasn't going to happen but I didn't have the guts to tell him. The final two were undoubtedly going to be actress Chelsee Healey and Harry Judd: it was their competition from the word go. The press were certainly saying it would be down to the two of them and they hadn't even considered Jason to be a runner-up.

We were called back for the elimination to find out who would be finishing in third place and when Bruce Forsyth announced us, I was ready to say how proud I was of Jason for getting so far. But Jason spoke first and said: 'Without this woman's vision and belief in me, I wouldn't be here. It is her outstanding choreography that brought us here and her dedication. We wouldn't be here without that.' I was so touched; I couldn't say anything! It was wonderful for him to say in front of the whole country how much he admired me and I was very honoured.

After that final show and after party, Joe drove us back to Wales and I slept and ate non-stop for two weeks – I didn't do anything else! There were two weeks to recover from the rehearsals before the *Strictly* tour started but I just felt so sick. I had a chest infection and was on antibiotics and I felt completely wrecked. And I wasn't the only one as when I met up with the dancers for the tour again they all said they had spent their Christmas in a similar way to mine – sleeping and feeling ill. I suppose it was worth it, though: that series with Jason Donovan really put my name back out there as a strong choreographer and dancer.

But it damaged my relationship with Joe, without a doubt.

I hadn't seen him for more or less the entire duration of the show, and although we spent a lovely Christmas and New Year together in Wales – with my mum too, which made it extra special – we both knew this was just a brief get-together. I had the tour to start at the beginning of the New Year and that meant another eight weeks on the road, dancing with Jason.

I think after that series I should probably have left the show. If I had really wanted to settle down with Joe that would have been the time to do it, to give up work and focus on my relationship. But I was so worried about losing my identity and just becoming someone's girlfriend. I didn't want all my hard work to be forgotten, I wanted to carry on working, and so I did. I was back on *Strictly* in August 2012, although we spent some good quality time together in between – we had some lovely holidays in Italy and Wales. By then I think Joe must have realised my heart wasn't in it and he was still caught up in a lot of negativity online, which didn't help. There were negative comments on Facebook and Twitter, and unfortunately he was vulnerable and was affected by them.

For the life of me I don't understand how people can be that nasty when they go on Twitter and just abuse another person for no reason. So why am I on Twitter? It's the quickest way to get a message across to fans or people who vote for us or watch our shows, and I always want the chance to thank them and send them a sincere message. Joe hated all the comments, he hated what people were saying about us, and I felt the same. We would show each other the messages and it was unkind what we were reading; some of them were very brutal – insinuating we were cheating on each other, etc. That sort of thing really does prey on your mind... it plants a nasty seed.

So when the next series of *Strictly* came along, I thought long and hard about whether or not I should do it. It wasn't that I didn't enjoy doing it, I just felt that Joe and I were fighting over little things and we were drifting apart. I thought to myself, 'OK, this is a job, it is a good job and it helps me support my family in Russia but I have to think about Joe, too.'

So I had to make a decision: it was either *Strictly* or my relationship with Joe. In my mind, if I agreed to keep doing the shows, the relationship would fall to pieces. But I also had to be ready to quit dancing, something that had been part of my life since I was six years old. I had to feel it would be 100 per cent the right decision. And I didn't feel it: I didn't feel that I was ready to sacrifice my work for my relationship and so by accepting the next series of *Strictly*, I knew this would potentially be the final nail in the coffin for my relationship with Joe.

I was partnered with *Bond* actor Colin Salmon that year and unfortunately it was a really weird pairing from the word go – he was 6ft 4in and I'm 5ft 2in! Why they put us together I have no idea, but I do know there were several queries from the audience as to why the production team thought we would suit each other. We certainly did click well, though – working together was good fun and we enjoyed each other's company, but it was just so hard to dance with one another! The Latin dances were OK, but the ballroom dances were impossible, really, as he had to bend his knees so much in order to lower his frame and I would have to wear three-and-a-half inch heels – the highest heel you can get for dancing! Dancing in those shoes for eight hours a day made my feet constantly swollen and I would have to put them in an ice bucket as soon as I got home. There was no way I could rehearse in my flats in training because it would be too difficult for him.

We were eliminated quite early, in Week 5, but I think Colin would have gone a lot further if he was partnered with someone more his height. He had great rhythm, being a saxophone player who knows music very well, and was very talented. I became good friends with him and his wife, who is a gifted artist. At one of our rehearsals she was doing little sketches of us dancing. She gave them to me and I still have them. When we got eliminated I thought, 'OK, maybe this is a sign.' So I decided not to do the tour – I wouldn't have a celebrity to dance with but I could take part as a company dancer – in order to spend some time with Joe instead.

I wanted to give us a chance to reconnect, so we went to Barbados and had a lovely time over Christmas and New Year with his family and friends. At that point I did feel that things were a lot more positive between us and we were back on track.

Then I got an offer to do a West End show with Robin Windsor. We were asked to be the lead couple in a world-famous show called *Burn the Floor*. The show was coming to the West End for four months and because they wanted a bit more interest when it was in London, they wanted a couple from *Strictly* to perform, so they asked Robin and me. Previously, Robin had worked with the Australian company and started dancing with them when he was nineteen years old. He had taken part in three world tours with them over ten years and then left them and came straight to *Strictly*. So for him, it was like going back to his roots, but for any dancer to get the chance to perform on a West End stage, well, it is a massive achievement and I definitely wanted to be part of it.

But first I had to speak to Joe as it was a big commitment. I told him how much I would love to do the tour and how much it would mean to me. He just said: 'Yeah, fine, you have to do it.' So I signed the contract for *Burn the Floor* and, in a way, I think I signed the end of our relationship. I would be doing eight shows a week at the Shaftesbury Theatre with only one day off a week.

So we barely saw each other; we were just like friends living together in the same flat. He was always going away to Wales or to other places to be with his friends, to socialise and go out drinking. When he wasn't doing that he was just at home in the flat waiting for me to come home from work. He told me that it got to him after a while – he thought that he was coming second to work and he didn't like how he felt. I understood how hard it was and we had a lot of respect and feelings for one another, but the love wasn't there any more: we had become more like mates and only saw each other one day a week.

Doing a West End show is very, very intense. You are doing eight shows a week that require you to be physically active throughout and it was really taking its toll on my body and on my emotional state. Joe and I barely saw each other and there was a big part of me that thought maybe I could have saved the relationship if I hadn't taken that last series of *Strictly*, or if I hadn't agreed to do *Burn the Floor*. Seeing each other for one day a week isn't enough, is it?

He said to me at the beginning of our relationship how much he admired my work ethic, how I was always wanting to go out and work and not rely on a man to support me. And he could see how careful I was with money and what it meant to be able to support my mum and aunt. He used to tell me how much he liked the fact I didn't want to be known as 'Joe's girlfriend' and just sponge off him. But that was at the beginning of the relationship and in the end my love of work became a problem. Joe just wanted to go on holiday all the time and drink with his mates as he had achieved all his goals in life; he had been the best of the best and now he could enjoy himself. But there was still a lot that I wanted to achieve as a dancer and as a performer – I never wanted to stop.

CHAPTER 21

Health, happiness and heartbreak

As well as having a damaging effect on my relationship with Joe, the show had quite a negative impact on my health, too. I was getting very dehydrated and I was dancing for two hours non-stop every night – and then there were some days when there was a matinee performance, too. It was a very hard four months and my health suffered as I picked up a kidney infection and had to be on antibiotics.

The first month was OK. It was tough, but I was coping. In the second month, however, I was struggling to drag myself out of bed. I had to have three cups of coffee first and I thought, 'This can't be right.' I thought I ate quite healthily – I had lots of chicken and eggs – so why did I feel so horrible? As a dancer, if your body fails you haven't got the tools to do your job any more. I had learnt the hard way about the importance of looking after myself: I ended up in hospital after doing the *Strictly* tour with Jason.

I had a few weeks off after that tour when Robin Windsor and I were offered a gig by BBC Worldwide to do a twenty-five-day tour with the *Strictly Come Dancing* band. It would be us with *EastEnders* actress Kara Tointon and her partner Artem Chigvintsev. We were all friends and the *Strictly* band was amazing – it seemed like the perfect job. It was a dream, especially as it was only for twenty-five days and we choreographed the whole tour; it felt very much like our gig.

But after doing twenty-five days straight, I was tired and although this was quite normal after an intense period of work, it was different to just feeling lethargic. I went to see a play with a friend but I had to come home as I was sweating a lot and felt very unwell. All I wanted to do was lie down and within half an hour of getting home and going to bed I had a raging temperature. I had a lot of pain in my joints and in my back, which I put down to muscle ache. But after a couple of days when my back was still bad and I still had a temperature, I realised it couldn't be just muscle pain. I would throw up after eating anything – even drinking water – so then I put it down to food poisoning, although my back was still bad and I had a severe headache, too. The doctor said it was because I was dehydrated and it was probably food poisoning I was suffering from.

I felt awful and I remember Joe and I were due to go to a charity event in Wales the following day. When we got to the hotel, I had to lie down on the bed and so I decided I would go to the event briefly, pose with Joe for the cameras and then come back up to bed. The evening was about to start and I felt like I was going to throw up in front of everyone so I went back to the room and lay on the bed. I couldn't move and so I called Joe (who had gone downstairs to make an appearance) and I told him he needed to call an ambulance – I was in agony. It was so scary, I didn't know what was happening to me; I just remember the pain was excruciating.

The ambulance took me to Cardiff hospital and they discovered I had a terrible kidney infection. I was so dehydrated that they put me on antibiotics and a drip right away and really looked after me. After lots of scans they told me that there was no lasting damage to my kidneys, which was good. When I spoke to my mum about it she said that when I was younger I had suffered with my kidneys, too, and that I would probably be prone to kidney infections. Apparently it is common in athletes and the doctors told me I needed to drink more water than I ever thought I should. I had to drink cranberry juice, too, to get some vitamin C, and give up coffee for a while as it was dehydrating.

So I spent the night in casualty and was on antibiotics for two weeks afterwards. It was a pain that I woudn't wish on anyone. I came out of hospital and rested and then Robin reminded me that we were booked to do a show on the Isle of Man. For the first time in my life I thought I would have to cancel a work commitment. I really didn't think that I would be strong enough to go but then I realised that not only were we dancing, Robin and I had to judge a competition that some children were dancing in, too. And I received an email from the organisers telling me 5,000 people would be in the audience, the local TV was scheduled to be there and the Mayor was coming. I just thought, 'I can't let these people down.'

Joe thought I was completely insane but I didn't feel like I had any other option. I had been out of hospital for ten days and so I went to the Isle of Man. We judged the children's dance and then Robin and I performed the cha-cha-cha but because I was so weak, I couldn't keep up with him and when he spun me round with his usual power I fell to the floor! Normally we are both strong dancers but I just didn't have the strength and so fell in front of 5,000 people, which was awful! But the organisers were really pleased with how it went and they were so grateful that we had come. I am glad I went as I hate letting people down; it just isn't me. As long as I work and I am needed, I feel good about myself. My private life has always come second as my love for dancing comes first – it comes before everything.

So when I started to feel poorly again during the performances of *Burn the Floor*, I knew I couldn't live through that sort of pain again and I realised I had to start looking after myself. But I wasn't about to pull out of a West End show as we were selling tickets with my name and Robin's name on them. Our pictures were plastered over the London buses and there were countless posters down Shaftesbury Avenue, too. I remember when I first saw my name on a London bus it was so exciting, I took a picture and I got on the bus. It felt so cool!

With all this excitement came great pressure and I realised I had to start looking after myself. I wasn't taking enough time to give my body what it needed and, as it was my tool, my way of making a living, I knew I shouldn't neglect it any longer. I was advised to do a pathology test, which is basically a blood test to see if you have any food intolerances. It's not about food allergies – that is different – food intolerance is about how your body deals with different foods at different times. When my results came back, I was absolutely shocked! Basically everything I ate (pretty much every day), like chicken, eggs, apples and bananas, I was apparently intolerant to. And dairy was also a complete no-no.

The doctor told me that when I ate those foods my body couldn't digest them properly and it created a lot of acid inside, which in turn affected my kidneys and liver. The acid targets the weakest areas of your body – which for me were my kidneys and throat. It did all seem to make sense: I would always suffer with a sore throat because my body was full of acid and I was eating foods that weren't good for my body. It was such a big wake-up call. Once I started eating the right foods according to the chart I was given, I felt so much better straight away. It was incredible the amount of energy I had as well.

Before, I couldn't get out of bed without having had a coffee, but now I haven't had coffee for over a year – I don't crave it now because my energy levels are much higher. I lost weight, too, and my body was completely reshaped – I felt like a new person. I think when I first saw the chart, because I was feeling so unwell and was so focused on getting myself better, I knew I had to stick with it. But it wasn't hard and I am quite disciplined: if I know it's not good for me, I will eliminate it. I have a big weakness for sweets and chocolates, though – but I do try to be good! Cutting out dairy made the biggest difference – I didn't feel bloated any more, just full of energy. I rarely get sick now. I'm not saying it never happens, but compared to how I was, this is nothing. It is astonishing how your diet can make you feel overall – I did a lot of research into what foods affect your body and how your body reacts to different foods. As a dancer you tend to neglect your body – you push it to its limits and expect it always to do what you want it to – but after so many years, it is likely to have had enough!

So I was able to continue with the show and when the run came to an end at the end of June 2012, there was a big closing party with the whole cast. Joe was with me and it was nice to share the celebration with him and everyone involved in *Burn the Floor*, but I knew it was only a matter of time before he and I had the conversation that had been hanging over us for a while. It was time to face up to our relationship. Joe told me how unhappy he was: he knew the new series of *Strictly* was coming up and once again he would be second in my life. We had started off in such a whirlwind romance – we were very much in love and committed to each other and it was a solid relationship – but I knew what he was saying and I couldn't deny that I would be caught up in the show again, so we made the decision to split up.

We both knew it was the right thing to do: we both deserve happiness and I will never say a bad word against him. He was a wonderful person to me and my family, but we fell out of love and you can't stay in a relationship out of habit.

The split was amicable; Joe was very kind and said I could stay on in the flat for as long as I needed as he was going back to Wales. He didn't want to release any sort of comment to the press but we realised, with the new series of *Strictly* coming up, that they would start asking about Joe and where he was. I went to Russia for a couple of weeks to get my head around the split. As soon as I landed back in the UK I had a phone call telling me *The Sun* would be running a story that we had split and someone else was involved. At that point we had to release a statement saying it was a joint decision, no one else was involved and we were still good friends. *The Sun* still ran the story and they also dredged up all the negative stuff about Joe using cocaine, which made me very upset for him.

It is hard to describe how I feel about having a man in my life. In one sense I am longing for someone to look after me and take care of me but on the other hand, there is a big element of trust. I just can't give myself to someone 100 per cent because there is always the fear that I could be betrayed and let down. That goes back to my dad, I suppose. It doesn't matter how close you are to someone, I carry this fear of being deserted from my childhood and I can never let that go. Our childhood shapes our lives so much and in a way, having been wounded, I am very much drawn to those who are similar. I think that is why I have become so passionate about my charity work. The charity Dot Com Children's Foundation (dotcomcf.org) had already been a part of my life for the past five years, but after my break-up with Joe I realised how important it was not just to donate my time, but to really get on board and raise awareness and much-needed funds for a cause that struck such a chord with me.

I met Sharon Evans, founder of the charity, the year I danced with DJ Goldie, in 2010. She works closely with Len Goodman's son James, who is a trustee of our foundation, and he had encouraged her to come and talk to me – he knew how passionate I was about working with children. I would always try to take part in charity events if I could and when I met Sharon she invited me to come to one of her events and to talk to the children about dancing. I was very keen to help and it was a wonderful way to use my status on the show to do something positive. Back in Russia I had loved teaching children and I missed being around them and their energy, so this seemed like a wonderful opportunity to help.

I was also very curious about the work Sharon did and after talking to the children about dancing and the show, I was able to find out more about the charity. Sharon's story was incredible. Her grandfather was a paedophile and had been abusing her until she was about seven years old. Her father was physically abusive towards her mum and as a child she was so traumatised that she struggled to read or write. Her mum eventually escaped that horrific environment and took Sharon away to an area with a local dance school. She went to the school and Len Goodman was her teacher.

Sharon said if it wasn't for Len and for dancing, she would probably never have become the person she is today. Her dream was always to be a newsreader but she had no confidence in herself and was ashamed to talk to anyone about her problems with reading and writing. So when she met Len she suddenly had a really good male role model in her life – someone to look up to and give her confidence – she said that dancing saved her. It made me realise how much in common we had and while I didn't suffer that level of abuse, for me dancing was also an escape and a form of saviour.

Sharon finished her story by telling me how she eventually achieved her dream of working as a newsreader, working for Sky and the BBC. But her career wasn't to last and one day when she came out of the BBC Studios she was involved in a terrible car accident and nearly died. She said to me that at that moment, the moment she was in the car and thought she was going to die, she felt that she hadn't achieved a purpose in her life. That purpose was to help other children like her. So she and her husband Neil created a charity to help vulnerable children deal with issues in life.

Neil was a policeman and he had nearly died in a riot the week after Sharon's accident, so they both felt extremely passionate about making a difference. They re-mortgaged their house to put this programme together, a programme called Values vs. Violence, which teaches children certain values in life. It is directed at kids who don't feel that they can speak about what is happening at home if they are being abused or bullied and they feel that they don't have a voice because they think they have brought trouble upon themselves. But through the programme they learn ways in which they can open up about their problems and how they can talk to adults about what is happening to them. Children can be so easily groomed and are often desperate to belong, which is why lots of them find themselves in gangs or criminal groups. The police see this programme as a way of preventing future crime and so it has been brought into schools to great effect.

The website dotcomcf.org was created by Sharon and Neil and I have met some of the children who have gone through this programme. It was just amazing! I met a boy whose father had died and his brother, who was autistic, could be very violent. This boy had so many behavioural issues stemming from his childhood but he went through the programme and excelled at school. Now he wants to educate other children and has become an ambassador for the programme. His mum wrote to Sharon and thanked her for giving back her son.

It was exactly the sort of programme I wanted to give more time and energy to, and I wished I had had someone like Dot when I was a child. She is the character Dorothy, who is a friend to all the children and the key to helping them open up. Children can write to her and tell her about their problems and if they are feeling threatened. She tells them that it doesn't matter who they are or where they come from: the most important thing is that they feel valued. To be honest, this is something that I am still struggling with: if I have no dancing, I am nothing. I have no skill, I'm not good enough just as a person because as a child, I wasn't worthy of love. My father didn't make me feel cared for as he left home on a regular basis. The only value I have is when I dance, and without that skill I am of no interest. It is something that I am dealing with.

So I started visiting schools in some of the most deprived areas of London and I had a lot of meetings with children, telling them about how I came from a small city in Russia and worked so hard to be where I am now. The thing that really struck me about the children with whom I worked was that when I asked them who they wanted to be when they were older the boys said football players and all the girls wanted to be actresses or singers. It fascinates me! The boys don't say they want to be footballers because they like the sport, but because they would like to have lots of money and become famous. And the girls say they just want to be famous, too.

I tried to explain to them that there is so much hard work, dedication and years of training that most people go through to become famous. I myself had to train hard for all my competitions and give 100 per cent to my career. If I wasn't good at my job then I wouldn't have been chosen to be on *Strictly*. I told them what I have gone through and the years of training and putting dancing first to get where I am now, and

I could see some of the children looking at me, thinking, 'OK, so it's not just that you wake up famous!' I tried to explain to them that if there was anything they felt absolutely passionate about then this was the time to embrace it. It's not always going to be easy to push yourself but that is what it takes to be the best of the best. To succeed – whether that's in football, rugby, dancing, gymnastics, or singing – you have to work hard. That is the message I wanted to put across. All the children see is the fame and the money and they don't see the bit before, the dedication to get to that point.

Some of the children came up to me afterwards and told me that their parents had divorced, leaving them feeling very useless, and that nothing good ever happens to kids like them. It was heartbreaking to hear such sadness, but I am living proof that it doesn't matter where you come from: if you believe in yourself, you can succeed. It's a hard concept for them to understand but I hoped that I was able to make them see that the surroundings you are born into or the people who live around you don't matter – it's all about having a belief in yourself. I think that is why I feel so passionate about the charity as a whole: I truly believe in it and I know how it can help, which is why I am a now a patron, having been a trustee for a long time. Of course there are thousands of worthy causes out there and Robin and I will always try and help with lessons or to raise money if we can.

It's not about publicity – I know there are lots of celebrities who will attach their name to a charity or a campaign just for the glory, but I don't believe in that. With beauty products, I am often asked if I will be the face of this new product or put my name to that. I have taken part in a few campaigns and if people ask me, do you actually use this product? I can say yes. Not only that, I can tell them why I use it, when I started using it, and why I think it works. I believe in a genuine approach to something like that.

I didn't relish the thought of spending the whole of July by myself waiting for the new series of *Strictly* to start, so I went to Russia to be with my mum for a couple of weeks. That did me good and I was able to take a bit of time out before the new season began – a season that I would be facing on my own for the first time in four years. It was time to be strong, and as dancing had saved me many times before, I was sure this new series would give me the focus I needed.

Now all I had to do was wait and see who I would be dancing with…

CHAPTER 22

Dancing with Big Ben

On the last weekend of August 2012, the professional dancers and the new batch of celebrities all met and were introduced at the BBC studio. We would be learning a big group dance over the next couple of days and it was a good way of seeing who was on the show, who clicked well with whom and how the celebrities and dancers looked dancing together. But again, we had no idea who we would be partnered with yet – that would be filmed for the launch show. It was nice to see everyone and they were all very kind and sympathetic over my break-up with Joe; they all told me I would be OK and I was very touched to have such support around me. The press were still writing the occasional piece about our separation but now it was good to focus again and be busy in my job. I didn't have time to sit down and cry any more: I had a new show to focus on!

Unfortunately those two days were a bit of a blur as I was also moving flats and so I had to enlist the help of a friend to help me pack. With two days of rehearsals from 10am to 6pm, there was little time for me to help so thank goodness she was able to be there for me. I had found a new flat to rent and I knew it was the right thing to do, to move out and move on. I don't think anyone realised just how sad I was about my relationship failing as I would always put on a smile. Whenever anyone asked me if I was OK, I would brush them off in a no-nonsense work-mode voice with, 'Of course, I'm alright, I'm fine.'

I was putting on this strong façade and it was a lot like being a child again and hiding how I really felt. It was, and still is, easy to bury my real feelings and just concentrate on dancing but the truth was, I was very down inside. Another relationship had broken down due to my love and dedication for my work. I wasn't sleeping very well either as emotionally and physically I was trying to pack away the life I had shared with Joe.

On the first day of that big group meet I felt exhausted so I went to find a spare room in the building to have a little nap. I didn't want to sleep particularly, I just needed to curl up and be by myself for about twenty minutes. Then one of the producers found me and asked me to go for a little chat with her.

'I am concerned about you, Kristina. I want to know if you are OK about doing the new series,' she said. 'I know how good you are at covering things up but you have just come out of a long-term relationship and we want to check you are OK.'

It was very kind of her to show such concern and I did open up to her a little that the only way I would be able to deal with the situation was because of the show. My biggest fear was that they didn't want me on the series and then I would have nothing – I would be completely alone and left to dwell on my sorrows. I wanted to work, I needed to work, I told her and so we left it at that.

I remember looking at the cast of celebrities that year and to be honest, I didn't really recognise many of them. The only two people I knew of were the fashion designer Julien Macdonald and the model and TV presenter Abbey Clancy – and that was only because they had a fashion connection and fashion is something I have a real interest in. At that point I was hoping I would be paired with Julien, being the only man I knew, and we had a little chat in the corner. He was really sweet and seemed really fun – he was the perfect height for me, too! The other celebrity guys, *Hollyoaks* actor Ashley Taylor Dawson and former rugby player Ben Cohen, looked far too tall and I didn't think I could be partnered with another tall person like Colin Salmon again!

Anyway, at this rehearsal the producers are there and watching how everyone gets along, and how the dancers and the celebrities connect and communicate. We rotate round and dance with everyone and I wasn't bothered in the slightest about who they saw me with, I was just happy to be there and happy to be working.

When the day of the launch show arrived people kept asking me who I wanted to be paired with and I can honestly say I didn't care at all – I just wanted to dance. I think a lot of the girls had their hearts set on the two young guys, Ashley and Ben, as they were good-looking men and potentially good dancers. All the girls were swirling around them. I danced with Hairy Biker Dave Myers and Julien for a bit of the group dance and I thought to myself, either of those celebrities would be great to be partnered with as we would have fun together and enjoy ourselves and that was what I needed.

I didn't really look at any of the other male celebrities. At the launch show I remember waiting with the rest of the girls to be paired up. Between the pairings there is the group dance and the professional dance and when I wasn't matched up in the first lot of pairings, we went backstage to get changed for one of the group dances. One of the producers came over to me and said, 'Kristina, you have to smile a little bit, it looks like you are about to be killed!'

And I thought to myself, 'I must be so focused on just getting on with the show and getting on with work that I have forgotten how to smile!'

So I apologised and promised them I would look happier. When Tess Daly introduced Ben Cohen to the audience and then called out my name to be paired with him I tried my best to look excited – even though it was a complete shock! We went upstairs to do the chat with Claudia Winkleman as it was the first year that Bruce Forsyth wasn't doing the show; it was now Tess as the main presenter and Claudia as the one interviewing the celebrities and their partners after each dance.

It felt like the end of an era, really. I had joined the show with Bruce Forsyth and I soon learnt what a huge legend he is in the UK. He was always so kind to the dancers too, as he had started his career tap-dancing at nine years old. He was very protective of us and it felt a bit strange not having him around although Tess and Claudia are brilliant together and great fun to work with.

After all the couples had been paired then came the moment

I was dreading: the press conference. All the publications, newspapers, radio, magazines… they were all there waiting to speak to all the couples as we moved around the tables and I just knew that they would all want to ask me about Joe and the break-up. I was scared: it was a genuine fear that no matter what I said they would make up a story and my private life would be back in the newspapers.

So we started moving round a couple of the tables and Ben was very taken aback that all the journalists were firing questions at me about Joe. He was a little upset that the BBC hadn't prepared him for any of this – that if he was to be partnered with me he ought to have been made aware of what the press would be interested in. Every single publication was asking me about what I was going to do now I had split with Joe and I did tell a lot of them that I just didn't want to talk about my relationship. Ben took me to one side and asked me what was going on and I explained that I had just split up with my boyfriend of four years, that he had been on this show as well, and that it was a relationship that had been in the public eye and I didn't want to talk about it.

And he just said, 'Right, don't worry about it.'

When we went to the next table and sat down and the first question was directed at me about Joe, Ben cut them right off.

'Listen, guys, we're here to talk about the show, nothing else,' he said, politely but firmly. And I was so grateful! Afterwards we went to meet his family, who were all there, and I told them that they were welcome to come to rehearsals any time they liked. Ben's mother, Lana, took me aside and said to me, 'Please look after my son; he needs a good friend.' And I said, 'Of course I will. We are a team now.'

Lana was very supportive, it was great to have her on our side and she was always very kind and friendly to me. She would come and watch us rehearse and I naturally gravitated towards her and I found her presence really comforting. She was so encouraging and even the following year, when I did the show with Simon Webbe, she would text me to say how well she thought I was doing on the show.

When the training with Ben began, I wanted to know a bit more about him – especially as I really didn't have a clue about rugby. I think it helps to understand where your partner is coming from and then I tell them a bit about my background, too. Otherwise you are just strangers and when you are spending so much time together, day in and day out, it's a good way to break the ice. After telling me a little bit about his rugby career, Ben told me a story that completely shocked me; it took all my willpower not to cry. It was the story of his dad, who had been killed trying to protect someone who was being bullied by two other people. Ben had started up a charity, The Ben Cohen StandUpFoundation Inc., in honour of his father.

And then I told him about my charity work and I said it is something I rarely get to talk about it as it is something the press are rarely interested in. It gets brushed aside as they are keener to get a juicy story about my personal life. We both found it fascinating that the press are always so keen to get the nasty things reported, the trivial things, but when it comes down to actually writing something positive and really important – and spreading awareness about a charity – no one can be bothered, it seems.

In Russia, helping people is a big part of our culture. When you grow up struggling and living in such a harsh economic climate, neighbours, friends, family – we all try and help each other as much as we can. It really is quite a sympathetic country and there were always lots of charities and plenty of opportunities to help people. I always wanted to do more charity work in my relationship with Joe – I was always trying to encourage him to do stuff as he would have boys who looked up to him and I had young girls who would want to learn a few dance moves. As a couple I thought we could benefit lots of people, but it never really came about. So speaking to Ben about his charity work was really interesting. I learned so much. He talked about all these fundraising events he had organised and how they worked and I thought to myself, 'I could help, I could do one of those for my foundation.'

Ben and I worked for ten weeks together on the show and during those weeks I went to one of his fundraising nights, an annual event he holds every October. I heard all about their anti-bullying campaigns and the work they do and I was happy to help by putting some dance lessons with myself up for auction.

I began to get very excited about what I could then achieve with my own fundraising events and working with Ben and seeing his drive for his charity really gave me a focus in my life. However a relationship ends – however amicably you break up – you still feel like a failure for not making it work. So seeing someone like Ben working so passionately on his foundation was very motivational and it did help me readjust my priorities: I wanted to concentrate on the important things like helping a charity that meant a lot to me.

Not only did Ben help give me an enthusiasm for charity work but, being an athlete himself, he was also able to give me an insight into the mind of a retired sportsman. Ben was a retired rugby player and he said that he understood what it must be like for Joe, a retired boxer, to come from a strict, rigid regime to doing nothing. It would have been a struggle for him and nothing would have been able to replace the adrenaline rush of competing. I know there are a lot of stories of retired sportsmen who go down the road of depression or alcoholism because they can't find anything to replace the 'high' they had when they were competing. Ben is a rare example of someone who has made the transition from being a successful sportsman to public figure and spokesperson for his charity, and he helped me understand how it must have felt for Joe.

Rehearsing with Ben was like a form of therapy session for me. I felt safe talking to him about my private life and how I felt – I knew nothing would get leaked out and he was a good listener, too. We were eliminated the week before the quarter-finals but being with someone like Ben, who was always so positive and able to set my mind back on track and teach me so much about charity work, was brilliant. I could not have asked for a better dance partner in that respect. On the other hand, I had someone who had never danced before in his life!

I asked him about why he wanted to do the show in our very first session, as I do with all my celebrities, and he just said it was because he wanted to raise the profile of his charity. Now that was such a heartfelt reason, such an honourable answer, that I felt an enormous amount of pressure to make him look good on the dance floor. He wasn't just looking for the next job, this was important to him and his father's legacy. Here was a big rugby player and dancing couldn't be further from his normal life, and I was responsible for trying to make him look good!

The cha-cha-cha was our first dance and he learned the steps really quickly, which was brilliant, and I felt a little bit of pressure taken off. OK, he was still a novice but he was picking up the right steps: so far, so good. Then I had to put the first few sequences to music and I realised something fairly critical about his dancing potential: he is half-deaf. In fact, over fifty per cent deaf, I think, so he can't hear the music fully, only the bass and not the melody. Not being able to hear the music is probably the worst situation you can be in as you can have the best routine in the world but the first thing the judges look at is the musicality and your ability to dance your steps to the rhythm. It is the same thing you are judged on whether you are on TV dance shows or in professional competitions, it's the first criteria that the judges look at – musicality and rhythm. So I thought, 'What on earth am I going to do? How am I going to get this big rugby player and lead him around the floor?'

He would have to follow my lead, there was no way round it, otherwise he wouldn't know what to do. Here was a big, strong former rugby player and we had to learn by me moving his frame around the dance floor. My arms and neck were in a lot of pain and people started asking me if I was doing some sort of weight-lifting regime as my arms had beefed up.

'No,' I said, 'just dancing with Ben!'

We didn't do too badly those first two weeks rehearsing the cha-cha-cha. He had learnt to follow my lead and I would signal to him with a hand-squeeze or something if he was getting ahead of the beat. And then the producers told me that we were opening the show on Saturday night! So we went on the dance floor and I just remember glancing over at him and he looked absolutely petrified.

'Please, please, smile,' I whispered to him.

And then a producer ran over to the side of the stage and tried to signal to him to just try and smile – that is all they wanted!

He did OK in the end but he was a little stiff and because he was then trying to smile he got ahead of himself a bit and I had to squeeze his hand so hard to try and slow him down! But he was ripped to shreds by the judges for being so ahead of the music. And I was so protective – I did remind all the judges that for someone who is half-deaf he wasn't that bad and to please give him some credit!

On the Monday when we met again for rehearsals we were set to learn the waltz but I don't think we actually got round to dancing at all as it was a bit of a therapy session for us both. He had found it hard being mocked by the judges and he didn't want to be made fun of. Once a rugby player and the best in his field, he was now in unknown territory and struggling. But I knew where he was coming from as I had been through it all with other guys on the show. I think it is very hard for men who come from a background of being really good at something to find they are not picking up a new skill as quickly as they might have wanted. Ben had come to raise awareness for his charity and if he was going to be booted off early then it meant I had failed him and not done my job properly. I needed to build up his confidence and belief in himself and after six years of being on the show, I felt I had become good at motivating other people – even if I wasn't always quite so good at motivating myself.

I had read a lot of sports psychology books and was fascinated by many of the motivational speakers, like Anthony Robbins.

When I first moved to America and started to learn a bit of English, I was introduced to the tapes. Even during some of my relationship break-ups, I went back to his theories about being positive. When you are on the show you realise how much your celebrity relies on you and they put everything – all their faith and trust – in you. Of course they go home to their families and they have wives or girlfriends or mums and dads to talk to, but in that moment, it is just you and them in that situation together on the dance floor and you are the only two people who understand what is happening.

Of course at the end of the day it is just an entertainment show but you still don't want to fail. It is a fear of failure, a fear of not coming across well or a fear of letting yourself down that most contestants have to deal with. And I think with men, especially sportsmen, it hits them hardest: they are used to being the best of the best and to hear any form of criticism is quite damaging and they don't know what to do with it. So on the Monday morning after the live show they unload on you and you hear all their fears and then they question whether they should have agreed to be on the show and how vulnerable they feel. Well, apart from John Sergeant, who just wanted to have fun – he did things his own way!

On the Monday when I met Ben after the first week I could just tell by his face that fear and doubt had completely taken over, so we forgot about dancing that day and just talked through everything.

'Of course you will feel emotional, you will be scared that the public won't like you and won't vote for you, but you mustn't give in to that fear,' I told him. 'You're obviously not a person who gives up as it wouldn't make you the rugby player that you are, you just have to give yourself a chance to go out there and prove you can do this. Both fear and faith are imaginary things, you just have to decide what you are going to choose to believe in.'

Thankfully, sportsmen can be good at taking coaching and I think I helped him believe that he did have it in him after all. From that point onwards, I think our training did improve. And I reminded him he was a novice and no one expected him to have an amazing technique right away. He was still learning and if anything, the audience love to get behind the underdog and love the idea that you are on, for want of a better word, a journey.

Ben took everything I said on board and stripped of his insecurities, he wasn't afraid to try things I asked him to do. Mentally he was better prepared and he trusted me and was focused on learning. As I have said before, by about Week 5 those who are still in the competition really begin to improve and that was the same with Ben. He really flourished and we lasted ten weeks on the show – not bad going for someone who couldn't hear the music!

I could not have asked for a better partner and when we were eliminated I was really upset. I was dreading this point; now I would have all this time to myself and be alone. As a workaholic, it was the worst feeling in the world. But dancing with Ben on the show and listening to him about his charity work was just what I needed and I was grateful to him for giving me a new focus.

As it was mid-November by then I asked my mum to come over and keep me company, and then we could spend Christmas and New Year together. So she did and now I had a little time off from the show, I decided that this might be the ideal time to try some therapy. It was something I had been thinking about for a while and in the end I found a life-coach to talk to. My very first session with her was an eye-opener: she couldn't believe that after all the things I had been through in my life I hadn't had any sort of therapy before. What she started to tell me made sense: she said I had been building up all this unhappiness inside me for so long that any little problem that comes into my life now seems so big I don't feel I can deal with it. In reality, those problems aren't that big or bad, but on top of all the sadness and past unhappiness, I was just adding to my overall baggage.

Working with the life-coach and having my mum around was really good for me and I was beginning to feel a lot more positive about life. I wasn't ready to start dating just yet, even though I had been asked out a couple of times. It wasn't that I still had feelings for Joe – I just didn't feel ready to see anyone. Mum was doing her best to persuade me to go on a date but I tried to explain that it was just a waste of their time and mine. I didn't want to sit down and make small talk or chat about *Strictly*; I just wanted to feel better emotionally.

Mum and I decided to spend Christmas and New Year travelling around Europe. It was a real treat for her as she had never been to Europe before. So we went to Spain for Christmas and New Year and then we went to Paris for four days to celebrate her birthday. I had travelled a lot through work or with a boyfriend so it was lovely to go to all these places with my mum and she absolutely loved it.

It was very relaxed and we could do just what we wanted. If I felt like crying, I could cry in front of her and we would talk about things. So as well as being a wonderful holiday for her, it was great therapy for me, too. I was slowly starting to accept who I was and I felt in a good place. I had the *Strictly* tour in January and February, which meant I would be busy again and when we returned to the UK in a sense I felt quite healed. Mum went back home and I went on tour.

I felt ready to stop grieving over past relationships – now I could just concentrate on being happy again.

CHAPTER 23

Charity highs

The 2014 *Strictly* tour was a success and as soon as it finished, I decided to start putting together my very first fundraising event for dotcomcf.org. Ben Cohen was very much on board and was a great help. He gave me all sorts of advice and information and put me in touch with people who could offer support. When I first got going, I called the chief executive and founder Sharon Evans about my ideas and said that we needed to put the charity on the radar by hosting a big event and to get the press on board. I started calling on all the contacts I knew and I think people were initially quite surprised about my involvement with the charity. I do it without wanting recognition and I do it because I believe in it: it's that simple.

And people did genuinely want to be of assistance as I never ask for help and for the first time in seven years I was asking! But I do have a lot of friends over here, people who are truly behind me and very supportive, and it was really wonderful to have everyone rally round.

I didn't realise quite what I was letting myself in for, though – the project just seemed to grow and grow. The first thing to do was arrange a date, so we put 19 September 2014 in the diary and Sharon organised Mansion House, the Lord Mayor of the City of London's home and office, as the stunning venue. That would bring everyone in, if nothing else, I thought. Then there was the matter of everything else to sort out. We had to get sponsors, a host, find an auctioneer, get prizes, sell the tables, provide entertainment… It did feel like a huge mountain to climb.

The biggest thing I realised was that the charity was still very unknown, so it was a case of speaking to a lot of people and holding meetings in person to motivate others to help us. But I believed in the project so completely and they saw that passion in me, so they really wanted to help. I knew that I had to put on some show-stopping entertainment too and there was only one thing that could be done: an evening of world-class dancing!

While I was planning and organising the event, Robin Windsor and I had a lot of dancing work to do, too. Mum was back over in the UK and so I invited her to join Robin and I on the Strictly Cruise that we do every year. It lasts ten days and my mum looked like a kid in a candy shop when we went on board! I suppose with her background in the shipbuilding business I could see why she was so fascinated by it all. And it was wonderful – although I did feel like I was the mother on the trip and she was the excitable child!

It was nice to be able to show her the world and take her to beautiful places. She was so proud of me and I was so happy that she could experience this side of my work too, and see that people enjoyed watching Robin and me dance. We loved the sunshine and the local food and she would go out in the morning to the buffet and have lots of people come up to her, telling her how much they liked me and how much they liked me on the show. It's lovely for my mum to hear such positive things about me and I remember her saying to me afterwards: 'I don't care how much the press get you down and write negative or depressive things about you, when you have all these people saying such lovely things about your work as a dancer, focus on them, not the newspapers!'

The cruise was at the end of April and Robin and I were solidly booked for several weeks in May, too, which normally would have been great. But Robin had started to complain about having a lot of pain in his lower back and he was struggling to stay on top of it. Actually, he first started to mention problems with his back in the November when he was dancing in *Strictly* and it was Blackpool Week. Everybody went out after the show to let their hair down (I stayed in the hotel to watch TV as I wasn't interested in drinking) including Robin and some of the other dancers, members of the crew and celebrities.

When you are out and about with other dancers having fun and a few drinks, you just start dancing even more. I wasn't there that night, but apparently, Robin tried to do a lift with one of the choreographers on the show and they both ended up on the floor. He ignored the pain (as I have mentioned before, being a dancer you just tend to dance through the aches and niggles) but by the end of the series he was still complaining about his back. And then on tour he was complaining, too, and that is just not like Robin at all. I realised something must have really hurt him, so I encouraged him to get it checked out.

He had to have a few Cortisone injections as he had a pinched nerve and was told his back pain was actually quite serious; the doctors said he might have to have an operation. But Robin, who was constantly in the gym and very strict about his diet and looking after himself, wasn't having any of it. 'I'll be fine,' he insisted. But I knew something wasn't right and I just had an uneasy feeling about it all. By that time we were both confirmed for the new series of *Strictly* and happy to be going back. We had been partnered on the show six years earlier and since then we had loved doing that job together. It wouldn't seem right if one of us wasn't there so we were thrilled to be back for the new series – especially as the producers had made some changes and brought in some new dancers. We were pleased we had still made the cut!

We had lots of bookings in June and July and with every show we did, Robin seemed to be struggling even more. A few weeks after it was confirmed we were both back for *Strictly*, he called and told me that he was going in for an operation on his back. Something had happened that day and now he couldn't walk. The situation was serious and he needed to have an operation to sort it out. I was heartbroken for him and I couldn't believe it was happening – how could such a trivial night out doing silly lifts back in Blackpool start this problem that now required an operation?

It tends to be harder for the professional men on *Strictly* to not get injured as they work with female celebrities who don't have dance experience and don't know how to hold themselves or support themselves in lifts. It just means they can get injured and overcompensate more, and then small problems quickly become worse. But as a dancer, *Strictly* is actually a small part of our year: we are self-employed the rest of the time and still have to find work. We can't afford to turn down anything that comes our way as we are the lowest-paid people in the showbiz world; that is well known. Our way of making a living is the work we do after the show: teaching, doing private lessons, personal appearances, etc. So I understood why Robin didn't say no to work: he didn't want to stop earning and take some time off to rest when he could still dance. Unfortunately, it was the worst thing he could have done and he was devastated to pull out of the new series of *Strictly* because of his operation. As a dancer, his body was his tool, and it must have been horrible to feel that it couldn't move how he wanted it to and that he had to have to have an operation – with no guarantees about what would happen afterwards. Robin is like my brother, my best friend, and I was heartbroken that I would be doing the new series of *Strictly* without him.

I tried to be encouraging: 'You will get better. You just need to get over the operation, get better and then we can get back out there and continue to dance,' I insisted.

'But what if I don't ever dance again?' he said. 'What will I do?'

Robin isn't just a great dancer, he is a special person to be around and a very happy, lively guy. He brought such a big personality to the show and I am very lucky to have had him by my side for all those years. He is such an upbeat, positive person, and our birthdays are only a week apart, which means we have quite similar personalities. We both have a strong work ethic, we don't tend to dwell on things and we were the perfect partnership. So when I started the new series of the show without him, I missed him terribly. He did come and watch the show a couple of times towards the end of the series, while he was still in recovery, and it was really good to have him there. But it did feel as though my right arm had been cut off. And it wasn't just me who missed him: the whole cast felt like a big part of the show was absent. He was such a funny, genuine person and was liked by everyone.

I started the new series of the show knowing that I had a month before my big charity event and yes, by that time, most of the organising had been done. I was so grateful to some of the dancers on the show as they had offered to perform for me on the night as the entertainment, which was fantastic. And the biggest support I got was from Anton Du Beke, who offered to host the evening. Anton is one of those characters who brings his own humour and identity to the show and it just wouldn't work without him. Only Anton could tackle such strong women on the show – like the MP Ann Widdecombe, for example (she would not have stood a chance without him, would she?) – and make it work. He has such a great personality and a real British humour – a wonderful sense of timing and wit. I really admire him and when I approached him to be my host and explained to him about the evening and the charity, he said he would love to help. I felt so blessed to have all my friends on the show help me and having never asked for any sort of help from them before, I was overwhelmed by their kindness.

The whole evening was brilliant. Anton was an amazing host and everyone was talking about how funny he was and how brilliant the dancing was. I partnered with Ian Waite, who was my knight in shining armour, and all the other dancers put so much effort into the evening. I also had support from lots of *Strictly Come Dancing* celebrities and the event was featured in *Hello!* magazine, too. I felt overwhelmed with support from everyone and we raised £93,000 in that one evening. It was just incredible! The only sad thing was that my mum wasn't there to see me do a speech, which she would have loved. I was speaking right after Cherie Blair and so I actually made a bit of a joke.

'I am OK dancing live in front of millions of people every Saturday night but how on earth do you expect me to follow Cherie's speech? How will I ever say anything more interesting than Cherie Blair?'

What I lacked in humour, I did make up for in honesty and I spoke from the heart about how much the charity meant to me. I was holding back the tears as I was talking about my childhood but the audience gave me a standing ovation afterwards, which was pretty encouraging. I kept thinking about Ben Cohen and how, without his guidance on the event, it would never have been a reality. He was the one who gave me the tools and the belief that it was possible to organise. I would never have found a way to do it without his encouragement, so being partnered with him was good in so many ways! I was very happy that he came to the evening, too, and it proved that with friends and people who believe in you, you can do so much.

It was an amazing night and a real turning point for the charity. And for me it was also a pivotal moment as I stood up on that stage and talked about my childhood. I no longer felt ashamed or sad about it, I didn't want people feeling sorry for me or seeing me as a victim; it was just about the genuineness of finding a charity that meant so much to me. I supported this cause 100 per cent, and when the fundraiser event all came together in September it was one of the proudest and happiest days of my life. But I was about to be brought back down to earth with a big, press-related bump…

CHAPTER 24

No good deed goes unpunished

What was a truly triumphant evening turned into a nightmare the very next morning. OK, so we still raised an incredible amount of money for the charity, but everything felt overshadowed by press reports about Ben Cohen and the breakdown of his marriage.

I think this needs some explanation. A week before the event somebody sold a picture of Ben and I to the *Daily Mirror* and made some nasty suggestions that something was going on between us. I remember getting a phone call about that photo during the launch of the new series of *Strictly*, and I thought, 'Well, there is nothing in the pictures so what is there to worry about?' We were on the Tube together, having just gone to the final dance lesson that had been won at auction at Ben's own charity event in May. I had auctioned two lessons at his fundraiser, and it was hard to get the winners all together on two specific dates so we ended up splitting the lessons into four different sessions.

There was a school in Kentish Town that we used for teaching those lessons. The owners were my friends and they let us have the venue for free as it was all for charity. Ben and I had been to the studio three times prior to this so we only had one more lesson to teach. There was a group of ten of us in the class and it was good fun, lots of the photos went on Twitter and everyone enjoyed themselves. I remember the date precisely: it was 16 June 2014 as I had had lunch with an MP in the House of Commons earlier that day. It is not something you forget! I was talking to him about the Dot Com Foundation and then straight after the meeting I met Ben in Kentish Town for the lessons.

Randomly, as we got to the studio, we met two of the producers from *Strictly*: the celebrity producer and the executive producer. We explained that we had auctioned lessons for Ben's charity and there was a group of people waiting for us. I wanted to know what they were doing there and they revealed that they had a few try-outs for the new series of *Strictly*. They wanted to meet a couple of potential celebrity stars to talk to them and ask them to dance a little. So we had a good chat, said our goodbyes, then we went and taught the lesson. After that we caught the Tube together, I went back home and Ben went back to Northampton.

I have put it plainly and simply because it was just that. So I was very surprised to get a phone call from my publicist in the middle of the *Strictly* launch to say that the newspapers were going to run a story that Ben and I were going on a secret date, using the picture of us on the Tube as evidence. It was absolutely ridiculous!

The headline said something like 'Strictly Friends?' with a big question mark, and the picture was just of me sitting in the carriage with my hands in front of me, chatting away about something to Ben. What was so weird about that? And the most damning point was that the *Mirror* had held this photo for three months before they used it – the pictures were taken in June, for goodness' sake! Then all of a sudden, when Ben's marriage being in trouble (which it had been for a few weeks by then) was in the press, the pictures came out. If they had appeared in June then I doubt there would have been a story around them, but they released them at the right time and I was then blamed for the whole breakdown of the marriage. The papers had made it look as though Ben and I were meeting around the time of his marriage breaking up and therefore I was somehow involved.

It was such a mess, and all just a week before my charity fundraiser, too, which meant that it just added to the stress I was under. So I hired a lawyer to sort out the damage such speculation was causing to my reputation, which of course wasn't cheap, but I was determined not to let the newspaper get away with it.

Ben rang me after the photos came out and suggested that it might be better if he didn't come to the fundraiser as he didn't want to give the press any more ammunition than they already had. But I told him that would just create even more speculation. Besides, it was Ben who had put the fire inside me to really focus on the charity and who had spent so much time giving me advice and support.

'I'm not a coward, you're not a coward, everyone who has helped me will be there and you have to be there too,' I told him. 'We have nothing to hide.'

So Ben was there and we were photographed for *Hello!* magazine and the paps outside the venue took pictures of him leaving the event as well. They used the pictures to add fuel to their twist on the breakdown of his marriage that I must somehow be involved. The articles were full of nasty allegations and I was shocked that our wonderful event where we had raised so much money for such a brilliant cause had been overshadowed by pure lies. It broke me completely. I couldn't believe this was happening and I was in bits – I felt bullied and abused in every single publication and magazine. But what is the old saying? The truth ruins a good story. It just felt like all they wanted to do was pile the blame on me.

It was the start of a long campaign of hatred, I felt. I was being slated in the press for everything possible. The *Daily Mail* put me on the front cover, deeming what I wear on *Strictly* as 'overly sexy'. But I have no control over the costumes – we have a dress department who tell us what to wear. Every weekend it seemed that something was being speculated on in the press and, in the end, Ben and his wife released an official statement that said there was no third party involved.

What made matters worse was that there were certain people who were regularly calling the papers and selling stories to the press. There were so many lies being reported I was torn to shreds by the media. I felt bullied with no support around me. Actually it was Ben who went on Facebook to defend me, which was brilliant. He said: 'It's a desperately sad world when two adults of different genders cannot have a friendship without being attacked maliciously. Stay strong Krihanoff. It's horrible being bullied each week for no reason at all. Thinking of you.'

I was grateful he said that, but it just added to the speculation and the press printed a story that the BBC had demanded a meeting with me to talk about my behaviour. The truth is I called the meeting because I was struggling and I told them that I needed proper help from the press office. I also wanted to reassure them that I was fully committed to the current series and that it wasn't affecting the work I was doing with my new partner, singer-songwriter Simon Webbe.

Before the series started, Simon had been struggling with a spell of depression and had spoken about using alcohol and his broken relationships quite publicly, so I knew he wasn't in a particularly good place either. It just felt so bleak. But I didn't want those nasty stories about me to affect him and, to be honest, after a month and a half of what I can only describe as abuse, I really did think maybe things would be better if I left the show.

It wasn't an easy decision, I thought about it long and hard, but ultimately I didn't want my negative press to affect Simon. He was very supportive, though, and he told me he had had his fair share of negative press and so he understood how I felt.

'Unfortunately, Kristina, you are just bringing more interest to the show and selling papers. You are strong, you will just have to stomach it,' said Simon.

Although I was very grateful for his no-nonsense support, it didn't make me feel any better. Around this time I had so much abuse online from internet trolls and countless vicious comments on my Facebook and Twitter pages. I was called all sorts of names, but I never responded. I remember one day I locked myself up in my flat, I didn't eat all day and I just sat and read all those comments about myself and I was just... I don't know how to describe it. It was such a low point in my life. I called my mum and told her that I was going to step down from the show – I just needed to escape.

I texted the producer to say that it was probably for the best if I left the show and that they find a new partner for Simon. I didn't want the situation to affect his results in any kind of way and I didn't want him to get any sort of blame for my bad press. I am not a selfish person and already we had been in a couple of dance-offs by that point, which I felt wholly responsible for: I felt like the public were getting at me by punishing Simon.

It all came to a head in Week 3 of the show. Simon and I had only a few hours to train because he was busy filming a new music video with his band, Blue. I think we only managed about four or five hours of rehearsing that week and the rumba, which we were performing, is hard for a male celebrity to learn – there is so much detail in the dance and the men have to show a lot of emotion. And Simon did struggle as he was worried about forgetting his steps and wasn't at all comfortable with the routine, which I had struggled to teach him in that time. So that week, when we found ourselves in the bottom two, I actually thought it was quite justified. But according to the press it was because of what I was wearing – a white shirt! As I have said before, it's not up to me what I wear. It was a reference to the film that the music we danced to was taken from – *Top Gun* and 'Take My Breath Away' – and I was on the front of the *Daily Mail* (where else?) under the headline: 'Viewers' backlash against Strictly Siren'. They said it was all my fault we were in the dance-off because: 'When it comes to a matter of taste, Kristina's routine and outfit left little to the imagination.'

And I thought, 'You know what? If I'm so bad for the show then just let me quit. I don't want to be in it.'

I was up all night crying and I didn't want to go anywhere or do anything.

After I texted one of the producers from the show about quitting, they rang me and gave me a bit of a pep talk.

'Look, Kristina, we don't want this to happen, we don't want you to go. We are dealing with a hugely popular show and you quitting will open up a big can of worms and the media will have a field day. We know you are feeling a little low at the moment but the press attention will pass and we know you will be OK. Simon is getting better thanks to you. Eventually people will stop talking about everything else and will focus on the dancing.'

The thing was, I was ready to go: I wasn't scared or worried about the decision, I just felt I couldn't do anything right. I sat at home and I thought, 'I don't want this any more.' I couldn't face the group dance rehearsals on the Monday so I cancelled them and then went to meet Simon to tell him I was leaving. But he was having none of it.

'Kristina, what are you talking about? There is no one else that can do the training you do, you are amazing! I work really well with you,' he said. 'And don't mind all of that newspaper crap. I have had my fair share of bad press and ugly press but don't let it get to you.'

It might all sound so trivial to some people. Why should I be so emotional about press stories over what I wore? But I was dealing with a much more sensitive problem than that alone. On top of everything else – and something no one else knew about – my mother had had a breast cancer scare. Petrified, she had to have lots of tests done as well. And the worst thing was, I couldn't be there for her. The whole situation was pure darkness – I could see no light, no relief in anything. I just thought, 'I don't want to be on the show any more. I don't want to be portrayed as a bad or nasty person in the press any more. I want to go back to Russia and be with my mum because she needs me.' The guilt that I couldn't be there for her was killing me but I was under contract and I couldn't just leave the show. The guilt and the press… it all got too much. And when I say that I felt suicidal at that point in my life, I truly meant it. I was having such dark thoughts and I'm not a person who gives up easily. I know that I'm strong but the abuse… it just destroyed me emotionally.

I couldn't find a single positive thing to tell myself, so what was the point? I felt a tremendous amount of guilt at not being with my mum and this black cloud over me meant that I would wake up and not want to go anywhere.

It seemed the only thing that had saved me before, dancing, wasn't going to be enough this time. But I had underestimated it; I underestimated the fact that I have such a feeling of responsibility in me and I don't like to let anyone down. I couldn't be there for my mum but I could be there for Simon and the show and prove to myself I wasn't a quitter. And that is the only reason I stayed: because I wasn't a quitter. With Simon and the producers' support, I got my head focussed and let dancing take control of my life again.

And you know what? It worked.

CHAPTER 25

Putting my best dancing foot forward

The next few weeks on the show gave us a real boost. We worked hard, we started getting better marks from the judges, and the comments were more positive. It didn't mean we were exempt from being in a few more dance-offs, however, but that was the nature of the competition that year – there was such a strong line-up of dancers. The further we progressed, the more positive the press became and I was happy that they were finally talking about the dancing – although it wasn't for long. Because as we all know, two young, single people dancing together must mean that something is going on. Lo and behold, stories started circulating that Simon and I were dating. I could not believe it! Actually I remember laughing at that point, thinking, 'You must be kidding me! I was just moving on from all the mess with Ben and now you are spinning a story that Simon and I must be dating because we are both single? Honestly!'

257

Immediately, Simon set the record straight, saying nothing like that was happening, it was all speculation. He said categorically it wasn't true and that we were just trying to concentrate on our dancing. And this was one of the first times I went on Twitter to respond to the stories: 'It's all lies and I'm quite tired of lies.'

My agent always advises me not to put anything on Twitter as it can be used against me, but I'd had enough by then. I didn't want to read this gossip and I'd had enough of it overshadowing my work on the dance floor. I will never understand how the papers can get away with writing such rubbish. And then after we made our official denials, the next round of articles appeared. Can you guess what they were saying now? Apparently Simon and I would 'come out' as a couple after the final! It drove me mad that they just couldn't leave us alone. Why couldn't they talk about our dancing? And what made it worse was that it pollutes people's minds with lies. Some people will read it and not believe a word and others will read it and believe every single thing. It was driving me insane, and by the time we got to the quarter-finals I had really had enough – I didn't want to be in this environment any longer.

The night of the quarter-finals we were opening the show with the American smooth and something didn't go quite right with one of our lifts. We just thought to ourselves, 'OK, here we go again, we'll be in the dance-off with that mistake.' And the standard was so high – with singer-songwriter Pixie Lott, presenter Caroline Flack, Frankie from The Saturdays and Jake Wood from *EastEnders* – you couldn't afford to make mistakes.

So we resigned ourselves to being in the dance-off, especially as our scores put us mid-table, which is a very dangerous place to be. As expected, we were in the bottom two and up against Pixie Lott, who is – and had been all series – an incredible dancer.

So while we were waiting to be told the couple who would be leaving, mentally I started to prepare my goodbye speech. And I wasn't just saying goodbye to the series, I was preparing to announce my retirement from the show completely. I'd had an amazing seven years but now it was time to say farewell and I was ready to let everyone know that I would be leaving. It wasn't a rash decision – I was almost relieved to be putting it together in my head. I could go and see my mum and support her, I could focus on what mattered in life. Now I would find something else to do instead of dancing. I was really into my choreography and I had choreographed a lot of the group dances over the years on the show. I was the only professional dancer who had been asked to choreograph the whole of one of the Christmas specials as well. It was the year I danced with Colin Salmon and I choreographed all the professional group dances and all the celebrity ones for that one-off show.

And saying goodbye to the press was going to be a blessing. I won't be the first or the last person to feel defeated by the media and I genuinely felt I was being forced out of show business by all the gossip and fake stories that the newspapers and magazines wrote about me. When I had appeared on *Loose Women* in June 2015, panellist Jane Moore had pointed out that because I had done interviews with *Hello!* magazine I was fair game. But the interviews were ones I chose to do; they were within my control. What I said in those interviews are things I am willing to share with the public. But because I do it willingly it doesn't mean that I then want thousands of negative articles or people digging into my private life every other day just to get an angle because they need a story to fill their pages. You can't justify my couple of interviews as a free pass for them to harass my family. And it doesn't give them permission to write all sorts of things about me either.

The show was brilliant for me but there was such a big price to pay. I think I understood where John Sergeant was coming from all those years ago because he knew how the press could be: he didn't want to put his family through the harassment they were getting and so he stood down. While I was standing there with Simon that thought zoomed into my head: 'I do not want my family to struggle with this any more, I am a better person than this.' I had given my best to Simon as a professional dancer and yet I was once again in the dance-off, the press were having a field day and my mum was sick, too.

And while I was thinking of all of those things, I suddenly tuned in to what Len Goodman was saying. As he was the head judge and the judging panel was split, he had the over-riding vote. Whatever decision he made was final.

And that is when I heard him say: 'In my heart, when I go home I have to know that I have made the right decision. And that is why I am saving Simon and Kristina.'

I. Could. Not. Believe. It. Simon collapsed on the floor and I couldn't stop sobbing. All the emotion spilled out of me. It could only have been a matter of seconds but it felt like an eternity and I just couldn't stop.

Everyone kept saying to me: 'Kristina, stop crying, stop crying – no one has died!'

But I was crying because I wasn't out of the show – because in my head I was ready to go. Simon was trying to calm me down. He kept saying, 'It's OK, we've made it through to the semi-finals, we did it!' But I couldn't bring myself to say to him, 'It's not that, I'm crying because I wanted to go!'

My professional side kicked in and I thought, 'OK, we've got to fight back now. Simon is just so happy we are through and I've got to be ready to give him my all.'

When we started rehearsals in semi-finals week, the producers came and spoke to me about what sort of things I had planned for the finals.

'You know what? Don't even talk to me about the finals,' I said. 'I'm not thinking about a show dance or anything else, I'm pretty sure we won't make it to the finals so why not just let us enjoy the semi-finals?'

But they were insistent. As a production team they have to think about things in advance and if there are any props or anything they need to know. To me there was just too much pressure and so I ended up blurting out all my worries about my mum.

'Do you know what I have been dealing with?' I said. 'My mum has had a breast cancer scare and I had to deal with that the whole time I have been getting crap from the press! I just want to concentrate on the semi-finals. Please.'

And I was so glad I told them because they were very sympathetic. I think it helped them understand where I was emotionally. Mum had told me in early September that she had a pain and now we were in December. I had been dealing with this on my own for too long. I needed to let them know why my head had been all over the place.

So in the semi-finals we had to do two dances, and you know what? Simon was amazing; he was completely on his A-game! I had now told him about my mum and he totally understood what was going on and was very sympathetic. He worked so hard and I just wanted to do the best routines we could possibly do to give it our all. We had made it through to the semi-finals despite everything – through all this stress, through all the dance-offs and all this negativity, so now we wanted to show we had earned our place. In our minds we didn't think that we would end up in the final, so we wanted to enjoy the semis.

We danced the foxtrot and it was just perfect. Len said that Simon had performed the foxtrot so well he might just have got himself a ticket to the final. And that was amazing to hear! We thought we had done a good job and we didn't care if we were in the dance-off at that stage: if anything we had proved we could do it and we were proud of ourselves. When Tess Daly announced that Jake Wood and his partner Janette Manrara were the other couple in the dance-off against former *TOWIE* star Mark Wright and his dance partner Karen Hauer, I just turned to Simon in complete shock and exclaimed: 'We're in the final!'

It's such a cliché but this had been a real journey for us both. I remember meeting Simon at the beginning of the series and thinking he was the kind of guy who was trying to be cool – he seemed too casual about the whole show. He had an attitude of: 'I'll be here for a couple of weeks then I'll go. I won't get myself too worked up about it'. But I think it was because he was very shy on his own. He had always been surrounded by the other members of his band and never felt comfortable going solo. The show helped him become more of an individual and in the end he fell in love with dance. He told the press how much dancing had really turned his life around – and his approach to life, too. Dancing is such a beautiful tool; it was always my form of therapy and now I saw the same thing happening with Simon. It changed how he behaved, how he acted and how he felt about himself.

And public perception of someone is usually so different to how they really are. In my seven years on the show, I am incredibly lucky to have worked with so many different characters. Each and every single one of them was so different. In real life I would probably never have crossed paths with any of them, but working on *Strictly* gave me the chance to meet some exceptional people. That is the beauty of the show and you create a bond with all your partners. I had an equally great bond with John Sergeant as I did with Jason Donovan. You see people for who they are – vulnerable, stressed, happy and sad. They are learning and growing because of the show and you grow with them. You become a team and you are responsible for the journey they have because they rely on you.

Simon and I were in a bit of a daze after Saturday night. We never thought we would be in the final and now we had three dances to prepare. It was ridiculous! We had to perform a new show dance, the judges' choice and our choice. The judges chose for us to do the Charleston and we chose the Argentine tango. I made our show dance a little bit crazy and difficult and Simon ended up saying to me: 'Kristina, you've put seven lifts in this dance. I'm not sure I can do this!'

And I made sure we had lots of props and costume changes, too – I was very proud of the show dance.

The final was a fantastic night. Simon and I wanted people to see that we were enjoying every moment and that we were grateful to everyone for being there. We closed the show with the Argentine tango and we put our heart and soul into every second of it. Every emotion was in there and we were so tired as well, to the point of collapse. I remember Simon saying that he hoped he didn't drop me out of the lifts as he felt he just didn't have the strength any more. And I was struggling to even stand up! We just wanted it to come out well and when we finished, the audience went crazy! It was the loudest standing ovation I have ever heard and the judges said we should both be very proud of what we had achieved.

In my heart, even though we didn't win the series, I had won it with Simon. Anyone else would have crumbled with the things we had gone through, but we just kept working hard and went for it. And I felt really proud – proud of Simon, proud of myself. I think that dance, the tango, will be remembered in the history of *Strictly*. Before I think the dance people associated with me was the John Sergeant 'drag', but now I have a good dance to be remembered for.

The audience certainly remembered it when we danced the Argentine tango on the last night of the tour at the O2. That applause I will never forget. It felt like applause for thirty years of dedication to dancing. And that is something the press can't take away from me: they can write whatever they want but they can never take away who I am, or the passion I have for my dancing, or my love for my family, or my dedication to my charity. My life has never been easy – I have had to fight hard, work hard and take chances, but all those things have made me who I am.

I don't want my private life to be a topic of conversation – I just want to succeed in my career because I have worked hard at it. I want people to feel that they understand my life now. This is me, the real me. I find it so hard to understand why I am on the front pages of a newspaper just because I am on holiday or because I am talking to someone. Why is reporting my private life important or newsworthy? I walk past a newsagents and I see my face in the newspaper and I just don't see how it benefits anyone. I will never understand that. It's no one's business but mine.

So, what does the future hold? I am pleased to say my mum had an operation to remove all those precancerous cells and recovered well. There were lots of tests and sleepless nights but she is OK. And our relationship just goes from strength to strength. I would like to be a mother myself one day. A family is something I have always craved and the older I get, the more I want it. And workwise, who knows where the wonders of dance and showbiz will take me? But hey, I am sure you will be able to read all about it in the *Daily Mail* – they seem to know more about what I am doing than I do!

One thing I have learnt in life is never to plan anything too far ahead. Life is crazy! As a Virgo I am a very organised person and it makes me anxious when I don't know my next step, if I don't have a plan. But life doesn't always work out how you plan it and you have to be ready to take an opportunity when it comes along. You have to have belief and a passion; you must be courageous and adventurous. You could be the most talented person in your field but if you don't have the courage to follow your dreams, you won't go anywhere. My dream was to succeed and be a professional dancer and my life has rewarded me. So dream big, work hard and be ready for an adventure. And don't forget your dancing shoes…